# ON THE COURT

NBA AND WNBA

# ON THE COURT

## BIOGRAPHIES OF TODAY'S BEST BASKETBALL PLAYERS

MATT CHANDLER

ILLUSTRATIONS BY BRENNA DAUGHERTY

ROCKRIDGE
PRESS

Interior and Cover Designer: Eric Pratt
Art Producer: Tom Hood
Editor: David Lytle

Illustrations by Brenna Daugherty, 2020. | brennadaugherty.com

Author photo courtesy of ©Mark Webster Media

ISBN: Print 978-1-64611-273-9 | eBook 978-1-64611-274-6 R0

TO AMBER, ZOEY, AND OLIVER: MY BEST FRIEND,
MY ZEE DUCK, AND MY FAVORITE BASKETBALL PLAYER.

I COULDN'T DO ANY OF THIS WITHOUT
TEAM CHANDLER.

# CONTENTS

# INTRODUCTION

At 5'7" tall, I wasn't destined to have a career in basketball—at least not in the traditional sense. Growing up, I could hold my own in a game of H.O.R.S.E. or Around the World, but I had no illusions of one day playing point guard for my hometown Boston Celtics. Still, in a different sense I did develop a basketball career, as a writer.

I began my career covering high school sports as a freelance journalist. It was there that I got my first serious exposure, up close and personal, to the game of basketball. Sitting in a high school gym on a Friday night watching two teams battle it out is a great way to really learn the game, and I did. Years later, when I became a children's book author, I put what I learned in those early years to good use.

This is my seventh basketball book. In writing each one, I have developed a deeper appreciation for the game of basketball and the men and women who play it at the highest level. It is this appreciation, and passion, for the game that I hope comes through these pages and gets you excited.

Have you ever debated with your friends or family who the best players in the game are? Have you imagined that you are a general manager and you get to assemble a Dream Team of the best players in the NBA or WNBA? That is exactly what this book is. I have put together my Dream Team of the best player from each position in the NBA and in the WNBA. Ten chapters, ten players. The best center, point guard, shooting guard, power forward, and small forward from each league, together on one team.

And, because choosing the best is open to debate, I have included three honorable mentions for each position as well. Finally, no basketball book would be complete without revisiting some of the players that built the game. Basketball has evolved so much over the years. The players are bigger, faster, and stronger. The rules and strategies have evolved (three-point shots didn't even come to the NBA until 1979). Basketball players of today could not truly compare to the superstars of a generation or more ago. That's why you'll find a "legend" for each position included as well.

After you read this book, I hope you come away feeling a spark of excitement for the game. I hope you come to appreciate the contributions these players have made both on and off the court, and I hope you learn a thing or two (or 10) along the way!

I also hope you use this book to start conversations with your friends and family. Nothing livens up the dinner conversation more than arguing who the best players in the league are. Debate who on my list is overrated, argue who I missed, and discuss what you think would happen if some of the legends in the book squared off against today's superstars. Could MJ outshine Steph? Would Larry Bird get the better of LeBron? Make your own lists, argue in support of your own players, and develop your own Dream Teams.

Most of all, I hope you have fun reading this book. I love my technology as much as anyone, but there is something special about sitting down with a book, turning the pages, and being transported to another place and time. Whether it is the electricity of sitting courtside for Game 7 of the NBA Finals, or the excitement as Diana Taurasi becomes the all-time leading scorer in WNBA history, I hope you feel the magic reading this book that I felt writing it.

# WHY THEY WERE PICKED

First, let's begin with acknowledging the obvious: Picking the best person in any group is nothing more than an opinion. How do we define *great*? Most of you (probably all of you) have never heard of Dickey Simpkins, even though he won three NBA titles. Does that mean he is great? Not necessarily. It means he was a reserve on the Chicago Bulls dynasty of the 1990s—a player in the right place at the right time. Charles Barkley didn't win a single NBA Championship title in his 17-year career. Does that mean he was a bum? Of course not. Sir Charles was an 11-time All-Star, a league MVP, and an Olympic Gold Medalist who is enshrined in the Basketball Hall of Fame.

In the following chapters you'll read about players who may not always be the statistically best at their positions. They may not have a championship ring for every finger, but they may have the "it factor" of greatness. You'll also see some people left off the list. Hopefully you'll find yourself yelling at the pages, wondering how I could be so dumb as to leave off a player you are certain is worthy of inclusion.

The NBA has been overflowing with incredible talent for decades. Today, the NBA rosters include 450 active players and the WNBA teams include 144 active players. Narrowing those numbers down to 10 total players was a daunting task. To do so, I looked at a combination of factors, including length of career, number of playoff appearances, championships won, individual accolades (All-Star Team selections, scoring titles, etc.), and the impact the player has had not only on his or her team, but also on the league and on the community outside of basketball.

Players who didn't quite make the cut were given consideration as honorable mentions. The legendary greats were measured using similar criteria as the current players. In the end, I measured the final selections based on one simple idea: If I were a general manager and had to win a single game, and I could assemble the best players to field a single team, who would I choose? This is my Dream Team, and I feel pretty good saying they would be unbeatable in a single game.

# JOEL EMBIID

## NBA CENTER

21

| | |
|---|---|
| **BIRTH YEAR** | 1994 |
| **BIRTHPLACE** | YAOUNDÉ, CAMEROON |
| **HEIGHT | WEIGHT** | 7'0" | 280 LBS |
| **YEARS ACTIVE** | 2014–PRESENT |
| **TEAMS** | PHILADELPHIA 76ERS |

Big 12 Defensive
Player of the Year, 2014

2x NBA All-Star 2018, 2019

 @JoelEmbiid

 @JoelEmbiid

## CAREER STATISTICS

(THROUGH THE 2018–2019 SEASON)

**158**
GAMES PLAYED

**499**
ASSISTS

**3,833**
POINTS

**309**
BLOCKS

**1,804**
REBOUNDS

1

# A FIRST-CHOICE PLAYER

Every basketball game, quite literally, begins with the center. From winning the opening tip-off and setting some early momentum, to banging bodies under the boards and wearing out the opposing players, the center is—pun intended—the center of any successful team.

If the NBA were to hold an expansion draft and add a new team today, and the team was able to select any players it wanted, Joel Embiid would undoubtedly be the center of choice to build a winning franchise around. Embiid, the young, carefree spirit of the Philadelphia 76ers, may not have the eye-popping stats of some of the other centers in the NBA (and he is still waiting on his first championship ring), but he offers a mix of traditional and intangible qualities that make him the best pure center in the NBA today.

# A DOMINATING PLAYOFF DEBUT

The road to playing professional basketball was a long one for Joel Embiid, and the road to the NBA Playoffs was even longer. It wasn't until April 2018, four years after he played his last college game as a Kansas Jayhawk, that Embiid took to the court for an NBA Playoff game. Even then, like much of his NBA career, his playoff experience was delayed by injury. Just a couple weeks before the start of the postseason, Embiid collided with one of his own teammates and suffered a broken bone near his left eye. When the playoffs began with the 76ers facing the Miami Heat,

Embiid had to sit out the first two games because of his injury. With Embiid on the bench, the Sixers split the first two games, setting up a dramatic playoff debut for the big man in Game 3.

Philadelphia was trying to break a lengthy playoff drought, and Embiid and his teammates knew that. Even though he was playing with a mask over his face for protection, Embiid showed no signs of bowing to the pressure. Instead, in the biggest game of his professional career, Embiid came out and was dominant.

Like all of the greats, he was at his best with the game on the line. In the fourth quarter, with just under five and a half minutes left to play, Philadelphia was clinging to a seven-point lead on the road. Then Embiid took over. Catching a quick inbounds pass, he dribbled through traffic, executed a nifty spin move, and tossed up a fallaway jumper, banging it off the glass and into the basket. For a point guard it would have been an impressive shot. For a seven-foot center, it was stunning. But Embiid wasn't done.

On the next possession, with a chance to extend the lead to double digits, the big man once again showed his power on the perimeter. Dario Šarić fed Embiid with a pass to the far side of the court. He went up and over six-foot-eight Heat forward James Johnson like he wasn't even there, draining a three-pointer and extending the lead to 12 points. At the end of the game, Embiid led all scoring with 23 points. He added seven rebounds and the Sixers won. Still, Embiid remained focused on the big picture.

"I was sad I couldn't play in the first game. We went through a lot, and to be able to be in this position, I'm really happy," he said in his postgame press conference. "But we can't be satisfied, we've got a big one [Game 4] on Saturday."

That focus was critical. The Heat never won another game in the series. But Embiid, who averaged more than 20 points in each game, led the Sixers to win the series, 4–1.

# FROM CAMEROON TO FLORIDA

Joel Embiid was born in Cameroon, a country of 25 million people on the west coast of Africa, on the Gulf of Guinea. He is the oldest of three children born to Christine and Thomas, a retired colonel in the Cameroon army. Embiid grew up watching over his younger siblings, Muriel and Arthur.

As a young boy, Embiid had no plans to play basketball. The sport was so rare in his native country that there were only two public courts. Instead, the Cameroon national obsession was soccer. Beyond that, his father pushed him to pursue a career in volleyball. By the time he was 15, Embiid was nearly seven feet tall—becoming a forceful hitter in volleyball made perfect sense.

"When I was 16, I was actually supposed to go to France to be a professional volleyball player," Embiid said in an interview for the NBA documentary *The Way We Ball*. Luckily for basketball fans around the world, that never happened. Embiid would soon follow another path, one that would lead him to the NBA.

Most NBA greats have played basketball their entire lives. LeBron James, for example, was just nine years old when he suited up for his first team. Klay Thompson, of the Golden State Warriors, learned the game from his father's teammates on the Los Angeles Lakers when he was barely able to walk. For Embiid, it was different. It wasn't until he was 15 years old that he began to play the game that has now brought him so much fame and success.

It's no understatement to say that the odds of making it to the NBA are astronomical. And that's if you live and play in the United States, where the game is so prevalent. For a young player who barely spoke English living in a country nearly 7,000 miles away and picking up a basketball for the first time as a teenager, the odds would appear insurmountable. That didn't stop Embiid.

During a youth basketball camp, Embiid met Luc Richard Mbah a Moute, a native of Cameroon. Mbah a Moute is one of the few who overcame those long odds. He was drafted by the Milwaukee Bucks in 2008. During the off-season, Mbah a Moute returned to Cameroon to host basketball clinics. It was at one of those clinics that he discovered Joel Embiid.

Embiid's size and strength, especially for someone so young, stood out to Mbah a Moute right away. He convinced Embiid's parents that their son had a future in basketball. With Mbah a Moute as his mentor, Embiid moved to the United States and enrolled in the same high school that the Bucks power forward had, Montverde Academy in Florida.

Though Embiid would transfer after just one year to the Rock School in Gainesville, Florida, he was firmly under the wing of Mbah a Moute and on the radar of professional scouts. He didn't know it at the time, but Embiid was less than three years away from signing his first professional basketball contract!

# A HARD-NOSED COMPETITOR IN THE PROS

After high school, Embiid attended the University of Kansas, where he joined the Jayhawks team. Life in Kansas was good for Joel Embiid. Immediately, he was an impact player in the 2013–14 season, averaging 11 points and more than 2.5 blocks per game his freshman year. The Jayhawks made it into the NCAA tournament, but an injury kept Embiid on the bench. At the end of the season, he faced a tough decision: Should he return to Kansas, post a fully healthy season, and improve his prospects for the NBA? Or should he join the growing number of "one and done" players who opt to join the pros as soon as possible? In April 2014, Embiid answered that question, announcing he was leaving Kansas and declaring himself eligible for the NBA draft.

Though he suffered a pre-draft injury to his foot, Embiid was still selected third overall by the Philadelphia 76ers, two spots behind his Kansas teammate Andrew Wiggins. While Embiid rehabbed his injury during the 2014–15 season—he didn't play all season—he watched Wiggins start all 82 games for the Minnesota

Timberwolves. It took Embiid two years to get fully healthy and ready to play.

While he was rehabbing, Embiid used his time on the injured list to study the game. At 20 years old, he had only been playing basketball for five years and had just a single year of Division I college experience. Like an NFL quarterback who is drafted and then learns the game while backing up the starter, Embiid's time on the injured reserve gave him a unique opportunity to watch films, study opponents, attend team meetings, and immerse himself in the game in a way that wouldn't have been possible if he were grinding out an 82-game season.

In the 2016–17 season, when he was finally able to play, the Sixers brought Embiid along slowly, playing him in just 31 games. Even in that limited role, he averaged 20 points per game and showed flashes of the brilliance that led the 76ers to invest a first-round draft pick in him.

His biggest night as a pro came on December 18, 2016, when the Sixers hosted the Brooklyn Nets. Both teams were off to a slow start that year, and for one night, the man they call "the Process" gave the Philly faithful something to cheer about. Embiid poured in a career-high 33 points in the game, including a pair of free throws with 12 seconds left in the fourth quarter that helped seal a 108–107 win for the hometown team.

Though his high scoring and rebounding were crucial to the win, it was a play that didn't show up on the stat sheets that energized his team and the fans. Early in the fourth quarter, with the Sixers trailing by one point, Embiid deflected a pass and the ball headed out of bounds. Embiid launched his seven-foot frame into the air, vaulting over the first row of fans and swatting the ball back to the court. As he landed in the second row, the fans held their collective breath. When their star rose from the seats and climbed back onto the court, the crowd erupted. In a blue-collar, gritty town like Philadelphia, Embiid had just endeared himself to the fans. He was more than just a shooter or a rebounder: He was a hard-nosed competitor willing to do whatever it took to win the game.

# DRIVEN TO SUCCEED, WHEREVER HE IS

Over his career, Embiid has proven to be a dominant basketball player and a valuable member of the Philadelphia community. Still, it may be his drive off the court that is most impressive.

Embiid walked away from college after a single season at Kansas. As a first-round draft pick, he was expected to begin a career as a perennial All-Star. But during a pre-draft physical with the Cleveland Cavaliers, it was discovered that Embiid had a bone fracture in his right foot that would require surgery. The good news was that the 76ers would choose to draft and sign him. The bad news was that he would miss his entire rookie season. His dream would have to wait.

For a young player just two years removed from high school, the situation was challenging. Embiid was being paid more than $4 million by the Sixers, but couldn't play basketball—the one thing that had driven him for the past five years. Any other player might have been tempted to slouch off, to get caught up in his newfound riches and let his game fall off. Instead, Embiid rehabbed relentlessly. He was determined to come back better than ever for the 2015–16 season.

Then, disaster struck again. Embiid rebroke the same bone in his right foot and the team had to announce that he would miss his second consecutive season. The 76ers believed it was a potential career-ending injury. With more than $8 million in guaranteed salary and another year of painful rehab facing him, Embiid could have let his dream slip away.

Instead, he fought. He persevered. He worked out, stayed in basketball shape, and allowed his foot to heal. It took him nearly three years from his last game at Kansas to play in his first game in the NBA. But Joel Embiid never quit. He never let his bad fortune define him or defeat him. He proved he was a warrior, and in doing so he offered a valuable lesson to every young fan watching the NBA: follow your dreams, and never, ever give up.

# BRITTNEY GRINER

## WNBA CENTER

### 42

| | |
|---|---|
| **BIRTH YEAR** | 1990 |
| **BIRTHPLACE** | HOUSTON, TEXAS |
| **HEIGHT \| WEIGHT** | 6'9" \| 205 LBS |
| **YEARS ACTIVE** | 2013–PRESENT |
| **TEAMS** | PHOENIX MERCURY, ZHEJIANG GOLDEN BULLS, UMMC EKATERINBURG |

WNBA Champion, 2014

WNBA All-Star 2013-2015, 2017-2019

NCAA Final Four Most Outstanding Player

Associated Press Player of the Year, 2012

Defensive Player of the Year, 2014, 2015

 @BrittneyGriner

 @BrittneyYevetteGriner

## CAREER STATISTICS

(THROUGH THE 2019 SEASON)

**212**
GAMES PLAYED

**347**
ASSISTS

**3,667**
POINTS

**636**
BLOCKS

**1,556**
REBOUNDS

11

# THE DEFINITION OF SUPERSTAR

Big, physical centers aren't supposed to lead the league in scoring. In all of professional basketball, no center has been a leading scorer for more than two decades. Brittney Griner is the exception. The Phoenix Mercury center has won the WNBA scoring title twice—in 2017 and 2019—and she added two Defensive Player of the Year awards along the way.

Her dominance both as a scorer and as a physical presence in the paint and menace on defense dates back to her college years at Baylor University, where Griner became the first player in NCAA women's basketball history to score 2,000 points and record 500 blocks. Griner was a four-year superstar at Baylor on both sides of the ball, winning countless national awards and leading Baylor to the National Championship as a junior in 2012. In the history of NCAA basketball, for both men and women, no one has more career blocks than the 736 on Griner's resume.

Going into the 2013 WNBA Draft, few doubted that Griner would be the number one pick. And so it was when the Phoenix Mercury selected the six-foot-nine center. In the seven years since, Griner has solidified her position not only as the most dominant center in the league today but also, arguably, in the history of the WNBA.

# THE OLYMPICS AT LAST

On August 20, 2016, Brittney Griner proudly stood on the top tier of an awards podium 5,000 miles from home. When directed, she lowered her head, and an attendant draped the medal around her neck. Griner and Team USA had won the Gold Medal at the Olympics in Rio de Janiero. She beamed as she held the medallion tight, a symbol of all she had overcome in her career and in her life.

At home, Griner's mantle is packed with awards—she is one of the most decorated collegiate basketball players in history and has earned plenty of hardware in her young WNBA career. But most athletes will tell you that there is something special, something almost magical, about representing your country in the Olympic Games. And for Griner, it was an opportunity she had passed up once before, making this experience all the sweeter.

In 2012, Griner was slated to be chosen as the lone college player to join the US Olympic women's basketball team in London. Griner withdrew her name shortly before that selection was to be announced, citing the illness of her mother and her commitments at school as the reasons for her withdrawal. It was a monumental decision for a college student to make: walking away from the chance to represent her country as part of a team that was heavily favored to win the Gold Medal.

"I am disappointed that I will be unable to participate," Griner said at the time of the announcement. "I want to stay involved in USA. Basketball and hope to again have the opportunity to represent my country in future international competition."

As with most of her decisions, Griner said she had no regrets about backing out. But watching Team USA receive their 2012 Gold Medals that summer had to be tough. By the time the 2016 Rio Games rolled around, Griner had established herself as one of the most dominant centers in the WNBA and was a lock to be a member of Team USA.

As they did in 2012, the US women's team rolled through the Olympics with relative ease. Griner had a solid showing, posting 78 points and 47 rebounds in eight games. In an interview from Rio, Griner talked about what it was like for her to finally be an Olympian.

"I love it. It's just different than playing in the WNBA. We're playing on the biggest stage possible, you're playing for your country," she said at the time. "Being around all these great players, it brings out the best in you."

# IT STARTED IN HIGH SCHOOL

Brittney Griner was born and raised in Houston, Texas. She is one of four children of Raymond and Sandra Griner. As a child, Griner had no interest in basketball or sports in general. Instead, she describes herself as a "daddy's girl" who preferred to help her dad work on the family car, a fascination she still has today.

"[I] loved being out there changing oil and tires with him," Griner wrote in a *Sports Illustrated Kids* essay. "My dad wanted to teach me those things, so I wouldn't always have to depend on others. Even now, I'll help a friend out if they have car trouble."

When Griner did show an interest in sports as a seventh grader, she gravitated toward volleyball and soccer. Her height and long arms (she has an 88-inch wingspan) made her a natural on the volleyball court. Before that, Griner had another athletic goal: to one day compete in the X Games as a dirt bike rider!

After her freshman year, the coaches at Houston's Nimitz High School convinced Griner that she had the talent to play basketball. She quit volleyball and focused her efforts on what was for her a completely foreign game. Unlike many players for whom basketball comes naturally, Griner described her early experience learning the game as incredibly challenging.

"I was so lost," Griner once wrote of her first year playing basketball. "Coach would say, 'Set a screen,' but I didn't know what a screen was!"

Her former high school coach, Debbie Jackson, told *USA Today* that once Griner dunked the ball in a regular season game, everything changed. "After word got out that she was dunking the ball, we had 15 college coaches in the gym watching practice the next day," Jackson said. After two years playing high school ball, Griner began considering a future in basketball. She had grown to over six feet tall and would later graduate high school at six feet two.

By her senior season, volleyball and soccer were distant memories as Griner honed her skills on the basketball court. For a young lady who didn't know what a screen was a few years earlier, Griner had come a long way. She began her senior year by blocking 25 shots in the season opener for Nimitz. Relentless hard work was paying off. That same focus, hard work, and determination would earn Griner a scholarship to take her talents 200 miles north to Baylor University in Waco, Texas.

# THE MOVE TO THE PROS IS SMOOTH

In 2013, Griner was widely considered the greatest NCAA women's basketball player in the country. With that kind of attention comes pressure that often hurts a player as she moves from college to professional ball. For Griner, however, the transition from the Baylor Lady Bears to the WNBA's Phoenix Mercury was fairly smooth.

She launched her WNBA career at home against the Chicago Sky. Veteran Diana Taurasi opened the game with a long three-point attempt. The shot rattled off the rim, and Griner glided through the paint to deliver a one-handed putback for the first basket of the game and the first points of her professional career. She followed up her bucket by immediately recording her first professional block on the other end of the court. The rookie finished her debut with 17 points, eight rebounds, and a pair of monster dunks, much to the delight of the home crowd. Griner finished the season averaging 12 points and three blocks a game, sending the Mercury to a return trip to the playoffs.

In the 2014–15 season, Griner built on her rookie success, starting all 34 games for the Mercury. She raised her scoring to 15.6 points per game and averaged nearly four blocks per game as the Mercury finished with a 29–5 regular season record, eventually sweeping the Chicago Sky to capture the WNBA Championship. Following the game, Griner held the trophy courtside and talked about the experience of winning her first professional championship.

"The fight, and everything we had to do to get this win, it was all worth it to hold this trophy!"

# A GLOBAL ANTI-BULLYING ADVOCATE

Though her career is far from over, Brittney Griner has further established her legacy in women's basketball as an outspoken advocate. Griner has talked frequently about being bullied as a child. Growing up taller than most of the boys in school, and preferring, as she once said, G. I. Joe over Barbie, Griner was subjected to cruel harassment by her classmates.

"When I was younger, it really bothered me," Griner told the *L.A. Times*. "But as I got older, I started caring less . . . I've learned to love myself."

Griner said much of the bullying centered around people mocking her gender, claiming only a man could dunk a basketball. She also faced racial taunts during games and on social media. In spite of all of the bullying she faced, just before the WNBA draft, Griner made a bold decision: She announced that she was a lesbian, a fact she had kept private during her college career at Baylor. That, she says, led to a whole new level of harassment. Still, she has no regrets about her decision to open up about her personal life. With it, she says, came a chance to advocate for young people who are struggling with their own challenges.

Griner says she gets several tweets a day from young people asking her for advice about dealing with bullies. Drawing from her own experience, she says she often tells them to simply ignore the taunts. "Don't worry about what other people are going to say, because they're always going to say something," she said in an interview with ESPN. "If you're just true to yourself, let that shine through. Don't hide who you really are."

That attitude has made Griner a role model for young people worldwide, and it is cementing a legacy as a global anti-bullying advocate and supporter of the LGBTQ community that extends her reach on the basketball court to a worldwide audience.

## HONORABLE MENTIONS
## CENTERS

### ANTHONY DAVIS

When the New Orleans Hornets made him the first overall selection in the 2012 NBA Draft, they knew that Anthony Davis would be a force to be reckoned with. In his career, the big man has earned six All-Star appearances, collecting the All-Star Game Most Valuable Player Award in 2017. He has averaged more than 28 points per game each season and saved his best basketball for the postseason, where he has poured in more than 30 points a game. Still, for all of his success in New Orleans, which included signing a five-year, $145 million contract in 2015, he knew he could achieve more.

In the spring of 2019, the sports world was buzzing with speculation as to where Davis would be traded. One thing was clear: He wanted to take his considerable talents to a bigger market. And the Los Angeles Lakers came calling. To make room, the Lakers traded away their headlining first-round pick, Lonzo Ball; seasoned players Brandon Ingram and Josh Hart; and three future first-round draft picks. Paired with LeBron James, Los Angeles clearly had its sights on bringing the NBA Championship back to Southern California.

# NIKOLA JOKIĆ

The man they call "Joker" has carved out a spot among the best centers in the NBA during his five-year career with the Denver Nuggets. Drafted in the second round of the 2014 NBA Draft (39 spots after Joel Embiid), Jokić has steadily improved each season, posting career numbers in the 2018–19 season, including 20.1 points and nearly 11 rebounds per game. Those numbers were good enough to earn Jokić his first trip to the 2019 All-Star Game, and justified the $148 million contract the Nuggets gave him before the season started.

Outside of his NBA career, Jokić represented his native

Serbia in the 2016 Summer Olympics in Rio. He led the squad in rebounds, steals, and blocks per game. The Serbs advanced to the Gold Medal Game, where they lost to the United States, earning Jokić and his teammates a Silver Medal.

## SYLVIA FOWLES

Greatness can be measured in many different ways. For Sylvia Fowles, greatness is measured in her performances on the biggest stage, when the spotlight is shining the brightest. In college, Fowles led the LSU Lady Tigers to the Final Four in each of her four seasons. She has also anchored three Gold Medal teams at the Olympics and appeared in the WNBA Playoffs in seven consecutive years, averaging 15 points per game and 10.6 rebounds. The ability to perform her best in the biggest moments has earned Fowles two WNBA Finals MVP awards and one league MVP trophy. Fowles also holds the WNBA record for the highest field goal percentage for a career, knocking down .593 percent of her shots through the 2019 season.

## LEGENDARY GREAT
## CENTER

## KAREEM ABDUL-JABBAR

The biggest basket of the 1989 NBA Finals was a bank shot off the glass late in the fourth quarter from Los Angeles Lakers center Kareem Abdul-Jabbar. His team was about to be swept on their home court by the Detroit Pistons, but the bucket by Abdul-Jabbar was bigger than the game. It signaled the end of an era. After 20 seasons in the NBA, his final basket left Abdul-Jabbar as the all-time leading scorer in the history of the game, with 38,387 points.

As he checked out of his final NBA game, the crowd rose and delivered a thunderous ovation. Abdul-Jabbar's greatness was such that every member of the Detroit Pistons stood and applauded their rival. It was the ultimate sign of respect for the man who is unquestionably the greatest center to ever play the game.

At seven feet, two inches tall, Kareem Abdul-Jabbar was built to be an NBA center. After a four-year career at basketball powerhouse UCLA, where he led his team to three NCAA titles, the Milwaukee Bucks made Abdul-Jabbar the first overall pick in the 1969 NBA Draft. While it can take a few seasons for most college players to adjust to the NBA style of game, Abdul-Jabbar became an instant superstar. Dominating his opponents, he won the Rookie of the Year Award and was named to the first of 19 All-Star teams. (Interestingly, when Abdul-Jabbar entered the league he was known by his birth name of Lew Alcindor. He changed his name the day after the Bucks won the 1971 NBA Championship.)

With such a commanding rookie season, fans wondered if Abdul-Jabbar would experience a sophomore slump. Surely he couldn't top a rookie season in which he averaged more than 28 points and 14 rebounds per game. They didn't have to wonder long. Abdul-Jabbar finished the 1970–71 NBA season by holding up the NBA Finals Trophy and the NBA Finals MVP Award. He led the league in scoring with 2,596 points, averaging 31.7 points per game, and earned his second straight All-Star appearance.

For Abdul-Jabbar, it was just the beginning. By the time he walked off the court for the final time in his career, Abdul Jabbar had collected six NBA Championship titles, appeared in 19 All-Star Games, and had earned six league MVP awards as well as two NBA Finals MVP awards.

Abdul-Jabbar's career spanned 20 seasons, and although he is widely recognized as a Los Angeles Laker, it was during his first six seasons in the NBA that he honed his game and built the foundation for greatness. He was an All-Star every season he played in Milwaukee. He was a fan favorite. And he perfected the "sky hook," considered by many analysts to be the greatest shot in basketball. At over seven feet tall, when Abdul-Jabbar would launch himself up in the air to deliver a hook shot, it was literally unblock-able. The grace with which he seemed to float as he deftly banked the sky hook off the glass and into the hoop was a thing of beauty. It became his signature shot.

While big men are often known for their power, Abdul-Jabbar built a career out of an unmatched ability to bang bodies in the paint, then just as easily ball handle on the perimeter and score more than any man to ever play the game.

# KAWHI LEONARD

## NBA SMALL FORWARD 2

| | |
|---|---|
| **BIRTH YEAR** | 1991 |
| **BIRTHPLACE** | LOS ANGELES, CALIFORNIA |
| **HEIGHT \| WEIGHT** | 6'7" \| 225 LBS |
| **YEARS ACTIVE** | 2011–PRESENT |
| **TEAMS** | SAN ANTONIO SPURS<br>TORONTO RAPTORS<br>LOS ANGELES CLIPPERS |

NBA Champion, 2014, 2019

Finals MVP, 2014, 2019

NBA All-Star, 2016, 2017, 2019

Defensive Player of the Year, 2015, 2016

 @KawhiLeonard

 @KawhiNot

## CAREER STATISTICS

(THROUGH THE 2018–2019 SEASON)

**467**
GAMES PLAYED

**1,123**
ASSISTS

**8,250**
POINTS

**313**
BLOCKS

**2,950**
REBOUNDS

25

# HISTORY MADE AT THE BUZZER

It was Game 7 of the 2019 NBA Eastern Conference Semifinals and the Toronto Raptors were locked in a heavy-weight fight with the Philadelphia 76ers. The winners would advance to the Eastern Conference Finals and for the losers, the season would be over. Kawhi Leonard had no intention of letting the 76ers celebrate on his home court. He wanted a second title, and on this night, "the Klaw" was not going to be denied.

With 4.2 seconds on the clock and the game knotted at 90, it looked as though Game 7 was headed for overtime. The Raptors had one last chance to win it all and, coming out of a time-out, they dialed up a play to get the ball into the hands of their superstar.

Leonard took the inbounds pass and broke toward the baseline. Just before the clock hit zero, he launched a high-arcing shot over the outstretched arms of Ben Simmons. The ball bounced twice off the rim, then twice more off the other side. It appeared to be moving in slow motion. Then, the ball gently fell through the hoop and the Scotiabank Arena crowd erupted.

Leonard ended the night with 41 points, none bigger than his last bucket, which propelled his team closer to an eventual NBA title. That thrilling moment cemented his place in history as one of the most clutch players in the game.

Players who perform well under pressure are said to have ice in their veins. No moment is too big, no situation too intimidating. When the game is on the line, these players want the ball in their hands. Anyone who knows Kawhi Leonard—who has played with him, coached him, or hung out with him in the old neighborhood growing up—would all say the same thing: He wants the ball.

Leonard has spent a lifetime overcoming adversity, managing heartbreak, and proving the doubters wrong. On that cool May evening in Toronto, with nearly 20,000 fans screaming at the top of their lungs, Leonard did what Leonard has always done: He delivered.

# FACING CHILDHOOD ADVERSITY HEAD ON

Kawhi Leonard learned early in life the importance of teamwork and what it takes to overcome adversity. Leonard is the youngest of five children born to Mark and Kim Leonard. Growing up with four older sisters will teach you about teamwork in a hurry. The challenge of five siblings coming together isn't much different than five distinct personalities coming together on the basketball court.

Leonard started playing basketball early as a kid, growing up in Moreno Valley, California, a city just outside of Los Angeles. Though his favorite sport was football, a passion he shared with his dad, Leonard developed early as a basketball player. Known for his larger-than-average hands and quiet demeanor on the court, Leonard left a powerful impression on his coaches. In a 2019 interview following Leonard's MVP performance in the NBA Finals, his former youth All-Star coach, David Williams, said, "He'd always challenge me. If you say anything was outstanding about him at that age, it was the fact that he played defense, and he enjoyed it."

As Leonard continued to grow and his skills improved, it soon became obvious to those around him that he was a special player who was destined for greatness. "When he showed up [at practice], I called my dad and I said, you need to get down here right now," Leonard's high school coach, Tim Sweeney, recalled in a recent interview. "I think we may have a future NBA player."

Sweeny got the opportunity to coach Leonard purely by chance. Leonard's mother was working on the day of his freshman tryouts at Canyon Springs High School and he was unable to get a ride. When he spoke to the coach about a second chance, he was shown the door instead. It was a hard lesson to learn. With no basketball, Leonard focused on football, playing wide receiver for his high school squad. But Leonard had a love of basketball. After his freshman year, he transferred schools, and that was when he connected with Sweeney. That move would take his game to the next level.

By his junior year, Leonard was already thinking about a college scholarship. He was dominating on the basketball court. Off the court, he worked at his father's car wash in Compton. Scrubbing and polishing cars was tough, but Mark Leonard wanted his son to appreciate the importance of hard work. It is a trait Leonard has carried with him to this day, as he is often the first in and last out of the gym.

Just when everything seemed picture-perfect for

Leonard, tragedy struck. His father was gunned down while at work. For Leonard, who was just 16 years old, it was devastating. He lost his dad, his friend, and his mentor. Yet, in the face of this unthinkable horror, Leonard did exactly what his dad taught him: He fought back. The very next night he took to the court and scored 17 points.

From being kept off of his freshman team to losing his father, Leonard faced his childhood adversity head on and poured all of his energy and drive into one thing: being the best basketball player on the court.

# THE HARD WORK PAYS OFF

After attending three different high schools in four years, Leonard wasn't a highly recruited ballplayer. Though he had plenty of game tapes to prove his skills and the scouts were in the stands at almost every game he played, the offers weren't stacking up. In the end, Leonard decided to stay close to home and signed on with San Diego State University.

Not exactly known as a basketball powerhouse, San Diego State boasted just four players who went on to play in the NBA. They were mostly journeymen, with not a single All-Star among them. But Leonard wasn't worried. His confidence in his skills was growing, and if San Diego State was where he would forge a path to the NBA, then so be it.

With an increasing number of players opting for just one year of college before declaring for the NBA draft,

Leonard bucked the trend and spent two years at San Diego State. He led his team to back-to-back berths in the NCAA Tournament, advancing as far as the Sweet 16 in his sophomore season. Leonard didn't put up the explosive offensive numbers of many first-round draft picks, but at San Diego State he displayed a balance to his game that drove his draft stock up. He tied a school record with 23 double-doubles in his final season, averaging 15.5 points and 10.6 rebounds per game.

Those numbers were enough to make Leonard a first-round prospect, expected by analysts to go anywhere between the 12th and 25th pick in the 2011 NBA Draft. So it was no surprise when the Indiana Pacers selected Leonard with the 15th pick in the draft. What was a surprise was that within hours of drafting Leonard, the Pacers shipped him to San Antonio in exchange for a fellow first-round pick (from 2008), point guard George Hill.

For Leonard, the transition from San Diego State to San Antonio wasn't difficult. He started 39 games during his rookie campaign, averaging just under eight points per game. His output, both offensively and defensively, would improve each year for the next several seasons as he got more comfortable with the pace and the power of NBA games.

Playing alongside Tim Duncan in a stacked roster, Leonard advanced to the NBA Finals in just his second season in the league. Though the Spurs were beaten by the Miami Heat, they would return the following season for a rematch. In his second NBA Finals, Leonard put on a clinic. He shot an impressive 61 percent from the floor for the series, including a career-high 29 points in a Game 3 win on the road in Miami, and a personal best scoring 20 or more points three games straight. Following the game, Leonard reflected on his success: "Year after year I just kept getting more comfortable with the players on my team, and they started believing in me, and this year we won," he said. "I just believed in all the hard work I put in."

Unfortunately, Leonard's success with the Spurs took a stumble. By 2017, he began to get bit by the injury bug, playing only nine games in the 2017–18 season. At one point, though the team's doctors cleared Leonard to play, he refused, opting to get a second opinion from his own medical professionals. Further rumors circulated of a rift with teammates. A players-only meeting was held and the message was clear: The players wanted Leonard back on the court and saw his absence as selfish. Leonard would never play another game for the Spurs. During the off-season, he sought a trade, and in April 2018, he got his wish: He was dealt to the Toronto Raptors.

Soon after the trade, the buzz began to build that the Klaw had no interest in playing north of the border and might even refuse to report to the team. Leonard had made it known that he preferred to be traded to his hometown team, the Los Angeles Lakers, but the Spurs wisely opted to trade the Finals MVP out of the conference.

Meanwhile, the trade was a gamble for Toronto. Leonard had just one year remaining on his contract. For a player who reportedly had no interest in going to Canada, it seemed unlikely he would be more than just a one-year rental. And as it turned out, that's all he was. Leonard left after a single season as a Raptor, but not before playing electric basketball, setting career highs in points (26.6 per game) and rebounds (7.3 per game), and carrying the team on his back to its first NBA Championship.

As he held his second NBA Finals MVP trophy over his head, the fans, the media, and the basketball world knew Kawhi Leonard was headed to LA. The only question was, for which team—the Lakers or the Clippers? On July 10, 2019, he answered that question by signing a three-year, $103 million deal to join the Los Angeles Clippers.

Ten years after leaving Los Angeles in pursuit of a dream, Kawhi Leonard returned home wearing two NBA Championship rings and carrying two NBA Finals MVP trophies. Not bad for a kid who couldn't talk his way onto his freshman basketball squad.

# HE IS HIS OWN DYNASTY

In the era of legacies in professional sports (the New England Patriots, the Golden State Warriors, and the Boston Red Sox, to name just a few), Leonard's legacy may be in his ability to move effortlessly from team to team and make those around him better. He is, one could say, his own dynasty.

Only three players in the history of the game have won the Finals MVP Award with two different teams: Kareem, LeBron, and Kawhi. Players so unmistakably great they require only a single name. Leonard won his first title and

MVP Award with San Antonio, and five years later duplicated the feat with Toronto. Most experts believe it is only a matter of time before he adds Los Angeles to his list of title towns.

In a day and age where players announce every thought in real time and measure their lives in online photos, Leonard is a throwback. He doesn't use social media, often avoids the celebrity side of the world he lives in, and quietly goes about his business of being one of the most gifted men to ever play the game of basketball. That's a legacy worth leaving behind.

# ELENA DELLE DONNE

## WNBA SMALL FORWARD 11

| | |
|---|---|
| **BIRTH YEAR** | 1989 |
| **BIRTHPLACE** | WILMINGTON, DELAWARE |
| **HEIGHT \| WEIGHT** | 6'5" \| 188 LBS |
| **YEARS ACTIVE** | 2013–PRESENT |
| **TEAMS** | CHICAGO SKY, WASHINGTON MYSTICS |

WNBA Rookie of the Year, 2013

WNBA Scoring Champion, 2015

WNBA All-Star, 2013–2015, 2017–2019

WNBA MVP, 2015, 2019

 @De11eDonne

@De11eDonne

## CAREER STATISTICS

(THROUGH THE 2019 SEASON)

**190**
GAMES PLAYED

**342**
ASSISTS

**3,853**
POINTS

**298**
BLOCKS

**1,322**
REBOUNDS

# FAMILY ALWAYS COMES FIRST

The greatest story in the life of WNBA superstar Elena Delle Donne has nothing to do with her heroics on the hard court. Put aside her domination in four years at the University of Delaware, her first-round selection in the 2013 WNBA Draft, her WNBA Championship title, two league MVP awards, and Olympic Gold Medal—Delle Donne's legacy should be remembered not for what she did on the court, but for the reason she spends less time on it than virtually every WNBA star.

Delle Donne is the youngest of three children. Her oldest sister, Lizzie, was born blind and deaf and suffers from cerebral palsy and autism. Lizzie has never seen her little sister play basketball, never heard her voice, and the two have never spoken—at least in the traditional sense. Yet Lizzie is the center of Delle Donne's world. Though she plays in front of thousands of fans, has more than a million followers on social media, and is a world-class athlete, Delle Donne would give it all up if forced to choose between her career and her sister. In many ways she already has. Most WNBA stars play overseas in the off-season, earning millions of dollars to make up for the relatively low pay in the WNBA. Delle Donne has turned down every offer to play in Europe. Her reason is simple and pure: family first.

"Lizzie doesn't know that I play basketball," Delle Donne said during an interview for HBO's *Real Sports*. "She doesn't know that I'm 6'5". She just knows that I am one of her people and a really important person in her life . . . and that's all I want to be."

A modern athlete willing to completely cast aside any ego, not to mention millions of dollars in salary and endorsements, in order to stay close to home with her family is remarkable, though Delle Donne doesn't see it that way. "I don't ever get cocky over basketball stuff. I can shoot a basketball. Who cares?" she said to ESPN in a 2019 interview shortly after she won her first WNBA title. "My sister has been dealt all these incredibly difficult cards, but still perseveres. She's always been my perspective."

For Delle Donne, basketball is just one part of her life. Her sister keeps her grounded. Lizzie keeps her focused on what really matters in her life. And she makes sure to never take an on-court accomplishment for granted.

# OVERCOMING INJURY TO WIN THE CHAMPIONSHIP

Sometimes the biggest nights of a player's career don't show up on the stat sheets. For Delle Donne, Game 3 of the 2019 WNBA Finals was a career-defining game. Her Washington Mystics were tied 1–1 in the best of five series and they were on the road to take on the second-seeded Connecticut Sun. Delle Donne had a monster Game 1, pouring in 22 points and adding 10 boards to give her team the series-opening win. But a back injury forced her out early in Game 2, and without her, the Sun rolled over the Mystics. The injury left fans wondering: Would their superstar return at all in the series? A postgame MRI uncovered three herniated discs in her back. Such an injury makes walking painful, much less banging bodies in a professional basketball game. But Delle Donne wasn't going to let her team down.

Despite the serious back injury, she returned to the court for Game 3 and delivered a gritty performance. Clearly hobbled by her bad back, plus wearing a face mask to protect the nose she broke two weeks earlier courtesy of an elbow to the face, she seemed to struggle getting up and down the court. Despite her injuries, she gutted out 26 minutes of play.

Her team managed a 14-point lead and with just five minutes left in the game, the injured star was still on the court and delivering. Teammate Natasha Cloud lined up a jump shot from the point. The ball careened off the rim and Delle Donne drove into the paint, snatched the offensive rebound, and delivered a quick jump shot to expand the lead to 16 as the Mystics fans began to anticipate a huge Game 3 win in the WNBA Finals.

With no time to rest, Delle Donne saved her best for the deciding Game 5 of the series. Still hobbled by her injured back, she was determined to deliver the title to the home crowd at Entertainment and Sports Arena in the nation's capital. After powering her team to an 11-point lead, on 21 points and a team-leading nine rebounds, it was fitting that with 22 seconds left in the game, Delle Donne grabbed the game's final rebound and brought the ball up the court.

As she crossed midcourt, she let the ball drop to the floor, embracing teammate Natasha Cloud as the final 10 seconds ran off the clock. She had done it: The Mystics were the 2019 champions of the WNBA!

# AT HOME IN DELAWARE OVER UCONN

Elena Delle Donne's six-foot-five frame, built for power basketball, was something she inherited from her parents. Her dad, Ernie, is six feet six and a former Division 1 basketball player, and her mom, Joan, is six feet two. Growing up in Delaware, Delle Donne was the youngest of three children. In addition to her sister Lizzie, she has an older brother, Gene. Delle Donne has said that playing with and competing against Gene and other boys was a big part of her development as an athlete. "I could do whatever I wanted as a girl, whatever my brother did," she says on her official website. "I could play against the boys and achieve whatever they did."

Delle Donne first began playing basketball, or at least playing *with* a basketball, when she was four years old. As her height exploded, so too did the natural expectations that Delle Donne would follow in her father's footsteps and play basketball. She loved the game as a child, and towering over most of her classmates gave her a distinct edge. But it wasn't an edge Delle Donne always liked. Standing out as a girl who is six feet tall in the eighth grade comes with plenty of disadvantages. In an in-depth profile for *ESPN The Magazine* in 2016, Delle Donne talked about being seen as a "monster" because of her height. She also reflects that she felt pressured by her height to play either basketball or volleyball. "With a woman, there's a general sense that she has to play basketball because what else is she going to do?" Delle Donne told the magazine.

Despite her mixed feelings, she did play basketball (and volleyball) and she excelled as an athlete. Elite athletes often receive college scholarship offers by their junior year in high school. Delle Donne received her first offer to play college ball on a scholarship when she was in middle school!

The teenager continued to develop her already rare talent on the court at Ursuline Academy, a private Catholic school near her family's home in Delaware. In four years at Ursuline, Delle Donne led the team to three state championships and earned an offer to play college ball for one of the strongest women's basketball programs in the nation: the University of Connecticut Huskies.

After initially accepting the offer to play for the Huskies, Delle Donne backed out and opted to stay close to home, instead joining the University of Delaware. It wasn't UConn—not even close. But it was the place where Delle Donne would fine-tune her game and earn an eventual second overall pick in the 2013 WNBA Draft.

# FINALLY, A CHAMPION

Following a stellar career at Delaware, where she led the program to 104 wins and an appearance in the 2013 Sweet 16 tournament, it was time for Delle Donne to take her game to the next level. The Chicago Sky held the second pick in the 2013 WNBA Draft and they saw her as the next face of their franchise. She wasted no time in proving they made the right choice.

In the 2013 season opener, Delle Donne lit up the scoreboard with 22 points as she led the Sky to a win against the Phoenix Mercury and Brittney Griner, the player chosen ahead of her in the draft. Her first game was just a taste of what was to come. Delle Donne went on to have a stunning rookie season. She averaged more than 18 points per game over 30 contests. She also became an instant fan favorite, leading the entire NBA in All-Star voting and being named the WNBA Rookie of the Year.

After reaching the playoffs in her rookie season, expectations were high for Delle Donne and the Sky in 2014. Unfortunately, a bizarre illness caused her to miss more than half of the season. Six years earlier, in 2008, Delle Donne was bitten by a tick and contracted Lyme disease. Symptoms of the disease often can resurface many months or even years later. The chronic condition flared up in 2014 and forced her to sit out a long stretch of games.

The next year, fully recovered from the illness that sidelined her in 2014, Delle Donne had her most dominant season. She was unstoppable on the offensive side of the ball, leading the league in scoring with more than 23 points per game as she helped the Sky post a 21–13 record. Delle Donne earned another All-Star Game appearance, a scoring title, and her first League MVP Award to cap the best season of her professional career.

In her four seasons in Chicago, the Sky made the postseason three times. But even with Delle Donne's outstanding performance, they were never able to win a title. When she was traded to the Washington Mystics prior to the 2017 WNBA season, her chances seemed to decrease even further. The Mystics had never won the WNBA crown and had finished the previous season with a 13–21 record. Still, Delle Donne was determined. It took three seasons in Washington, but as she promised when she arrived, Delle Donne delivered the WNBA Championship in a five-game, thrilling series against the Connecticut Sun.

For a player who had suffered numerous setbacks over her young career—a serious knee injury, a hand surgery, a concussion, Lyme disease, herniated discs in her back, and a broken nose—winning the WNBA Championship was the culmination of years of literal blood, sweat, and tears.

# AN ADVOCATE FOR EQUALITY

Though still in her prime, Delle Donne has already established a deep, multilayered legacy thanks to her on-court accomplishments: WNBA Champion, league MVP, perennial All-Star, and one of the most dominant women to ever play the game. But, as with her unselfish love for her sister, Lizzie, Delle Donne's biggest legacy may endure off the court.

In 2017, Delle Donne married her longtime girlfriend, Amanda Clifton. She shared the engagement with the world a year earlier in an article in *Vogue* magazine. It was her first public acknowledgment that she was a lesbian, and for young people who looked up to the WNBA star, it was encouraging and inspiring. Delle Donne has used her celebrity status to advocate for LGBTQ issues and to fight for equality for all.

She also launched the Elena Delle Donne Charitable Foundation, a nonprofit dedicated to supporting two causes close to her heart: people with special needs and research for Lyme disease. She further supports the efforts of special needs athletes by running the Delle Donne Skills Academy basketball camp, where able-bodied athletes compete alongside Special Olympic athletes. "There's no greater feeling than getting to spend time with them and see them work with one another, and the joy of sport," she told Maverick Carter in a 2018 interview.

Perhaps Delle Donne's biggest impact is her determination to show that female athletes are every bit as valuable as their male counterparts—and that their value extends well beyond their playing careers. "Women aren't valued the same way men are in the workforce," she said during a 2018 television appearance. "It gets frustrating, but you've just got to continue to fight the battle."

Unlike other WNBA players, she has thus far refused to play overseas. Instead, she works tirelessly to advocate for higher WNBA salaries, so her teammates can enjoy the same off-season time to rest and recover that NBA players enjoy. It is a role she sees herself continuing long after she has hung her sneakers up.

Fans may see Elena Delle Donne as one of the greatest to ever play the game of basketball. She is much more than that. She is a role model, advocate, author, speaker, brand ambassador, and champion for women. Above all, she is someone who has refused to be identified solely by her athletic success, instead identifying basketball not as who she is, but as an important part of the bigger person she has become.

# HONORABLE MENTIONS
## SMALL FORWARDS

## *JIMMY BUTLER*

Jimmy Butler is something of an anomaly: He is one of the best small forwards in the game, yet Butler has played for four NBA teams since 2017. Originally drafted by the Chicago Bulls in 2011, Butler was traded away to the Minnesota Timberwolves, and has since spent one season with the Philadelphia 76ers and one season with the Miami Heat.

He averaged more than 20 points per game in five of his first eight seasons, earning four trips to the All-Star Game. Butler has seen his productivity drop as he has bounced from team to team, but he earns a spot on this list for one reason: He is a winner. He has appeared in the playoffs every season he has been in the league.

As much as he loves the game and as talented as he is on the hardwood, Butler sees himself as more than just a basketball player. "Life isn't always about basketball," he said during an interview shortly after signing with the Miami Heat. "It's about principle. It's about character. It's about so many different things."

In an era where so many athletes are consumed with fame and fortune, Butler has managed to deliver on the court and stay balanced off of it.

# KLAY THOMPSON

It can be easy for a player to get lost in the crowd of talent playing for the Golden State Warriors. Klay Thompson has spent much of his career in the shadows of Steph Curry, Kevin Durant, and Draymond Green. Still, Thompson has proven himself to be one of the deadliest three-point shooters in the league and as clutch a player as anyone in the game today.

Thompson's three-point game is unquestioned, but on an early-season Monday in 2018, he took it to the next level. Thompson and the Warriors were in Chicago to take on the Bulls, and Thompson had the hot hand. That night, he set an NBA record with 14 three-pointers in the game, finishing with 52 points. And he didn't even play in the fourth quarter!

But that was the second NBA record Thompson earned while showcasing his scoring skills. The first came in 2015, when he set a record for most points scored in a quarter. He lit up the Sacramento Kings for 37 points in the third quarter of his team's 126–101 win.

Thompson's stellar offensive skills plus his popularity as a teammate combined to earn him a five-year, $190 million "max contract" from Golden State in the summer of 2019.

# MAYA MOORE

Maya Moore was a standout at the basketball power-house University of Connecticut before being selected by the Minnesota Lynx with the first overall pick in the 2011 WNBA Draft. Since then Moore has done nothing but be impressive. In her first eight seasons, Moore has collected four WNBA titles and a pair of Olympic Gold Medals. She has also succeeded overseas.

In a 2018 interview with *Slam* magazine, Moore offered some advice to fans who wonder what it takes to reach the level of success she has enjoyed in her professional career. "To do anything great, you have to have a passion for what you're doing," she said. "You definitely have to have meaning in what you're doing and finding purpose in what you're doing. As long as I feel like I'm doing what I'm being called to do, then I know I'm where I'm supposed to be."

Moore's passion for the game was never more evident than in Game 3 of the 2015 WNBA Finals. Her Lynx were tied 77–77 with the Indiana Fever. With just 1.4 seconds left in the game, Moore caught a pass. She then smartly avoided the defender, went airborne, and buried the game-winning three-pointer at the buzzer! The Lynx went on to win the third of Moore's four championship titles.

# LEGENDARY GREAT
## SMALL FORWARD

### *LARRY BIRD*

It would be impossible to single out a greatest moment, or perhaps even a greatest game, in the Hall of Fame career of Boston Celtics legend Larry Bird. But if pressed, a case could be made for May 13, 1984. The Celtics were deadlocked 3–3 in the Eastern Conference Semifinals versus the New York Knicks. Larry Bird took the home court, looking to clinch Game 7 and advance his team to face the Milwaukee Bucks.

The Celtics won the opening tip-off and Bird wasted no time making his presence felt. Catching a pass on the baseline, Bird left his feet and buried a fadeaway jump shot for the first points of the game. From then on, Larry Legend, as he was nicknamed, went on to post one of the most commanding postseason games of his career. Bird drained 39 points and added 12 boards and 10 assists for a triple-double, sending the Knicks packing and moving his Celtics closer to winning the NBA Championship title. It was the second of the three titles Bird would win in his 13-year career, all spent with the Celtics.

Bird was known for his toughness on the court and his ability to make circus shots that seemed impossible. In the mid-1980s, no basketball player was more dominant than the man players affectionately referred to as "the Hick from French Lick" (a reference to Bird's hometown of French

Lick, Indiana). Bird accomplished something that only two other basketball greats (Wilt Chamberlain and Bill Russell) have achieved: He won the NBA MVP Award for three consecutive seasons (1984–86). Not even Michael Jordan, Kobe Bryant, Shaquille O'Neal, Kareem Abdul-Jabbar, or Magic Johnson were able to pull this off.

Bird was the centerpiece of the Celtics dynasty of the 1980s, alongside Robert Parish, Kevin McHale, and Dennis Johnson. Together, they collected three championship rings. But it was a cross-country rivalry that was one of the most compelling aspects of Bird's career. The Boston Celtics and Los Angeles Lakers enjoyed a spirited rivalry in the '80s and the two faces of the franchises, Larry Bird and Magic Johnson, personified that rivalry.

Though they would later appear in television commercials together, selling everything from hamburgers to sneakers, and speak of each other warmly as friends, at the peak of the rivalry, they were fierce competitors. Bird vs. Johnson was must-see TV anytime the Celtics and Lakers matched up.

Bird's career was cut short by a recurring back injury that required multiple surgeries. But before he called it quits, Larry Legend earned 12 All-Star appearances to go along with his three NBA titles and three MVP awards. He was also a member of the historic 1992 US Olympic basketball team, dubbed "the Dream Team." Playing alongside Magic Johnson and Michael Jordan, Bird collected a Gold Medal as the Americans swept through the Olympics.

In 1998, Bird was elected to the Naismith Memorial Basketball Hall of Fame. His jersey number 33 was retired and hangs from the rafters in Boston. In a city home to such sports legends as Ted Williams, Babe Ruth, Bobby Orr, Bill Russell, and Tom Brady, Larry Bird remains one of the most accomplished—and most popular—athletes to ever represent Boston.

# LeBRON JAMES

## NBA POWER FORWARD 23

| | |
|---|---|
| **BIRTH YEAR** | 1984 |
| **BIRTHPLACE** | AKRON, OHIO |
| **HEIGHT \| WEIGHT** | 6'9" \| 250 LBS |
| **YEARS ACTIVE** | 2003–PRESENT |
| **TEAMS** | CLEVELAND CAVALIERS, MIAMI HEAT, LOS ANGELES LAKERS |

NBA Rookie of the Year, 2004

NBA Finals MVP, 2012, 2013, 2016

NBA MVP, 2009, 2010, 2012, 2013

NBA All-Star, 2005–2019

NBA Scoring Champion, 2008

USA Basketball Male Athlete of the Year, 2012

McDonald's All-American Game MVP, 2003

 @KingJames

 @KingJames

## CAREER STATISTICS

(THROUGH THE 2018–2019 SEASON)

**1,198**
GAMES PLAYED

**8,662**
ASSISTS

**32,543**
POINTS

**921**
BLOCKS

**8,880**
REBOUNDS

51

# TRULY A KING

A case could be made (and was made quite aggressively by people in my circle of sports enthusiasts) that the inclusion of LeBron James as the best *active* NBA player at his position is flat out wrong. He has been the greatest, the argument goes, but now he is in his mid-thirties, his body has more than 17 NBA seasons of wear and tear on it, and he is more of a "very good" player today, as opposed to the best at his position.

It was thought by some that this title should belong to Brooklyn Nets forward Kevin Durant. His resume is no doubt worthy: He has two NBA Championship titles, two Finals MVP awards, one league MVP Award, 10 NBA All-Star appearances, and he's a former Rookie of the Year. Durant's presence on the court can instantly change the tempo of a game and the strategy of the opposing team. Likewise, his absence, as fans saw in the 2019 NBA Finals, when he went down with a calf injury and later a torn Achilles tendon, can leave a gaping hole in his team.

Still, there is something about leaving out the greatest player in the history of the game—who is still starting, still averaging nearly 26 points per game, and still fighting to win the NBA title with his third team—that feels wrong. Whether in Cleveland, Miami, back in Cleveland, or now in Los Angeles, wherever he has gone since stepping onto an NBA court as a fresh-faced 18-year-old, LeBron James has made an incredible impact on the game.

Like Tiger Woods in golf, James is the athlete with the rare ability to make people who aren't even fans of the game tune in and watch. His talent on the court, his charisma, and his leadership are legendary. Fans (and non-fans) know that every time James takes the court, history may be made. For instance, take the night in 2019 when James set an NBA record as the first player to record a triple-double against every team in the league. Or the night in 2014 when he poured in a career-high 61 points against the Charlotte Bobcats. Or any of the seemingly endless dominating performances of his postseason career.

James is special. He is more than a talent on the basketball court that defines a generation. He very well may be not only the greatest to ever play the game, but also the greatest that *will* ever play the game. He is, as a newspaper first dubbed him while in high school, "King James."

# CARRYING HIS TEAM TO THE TITLE

How do you choose the greatest moment of a career defined by great moments? How do you select the greatest game from 17 seasons filled with greatest games? What's your favorite LeBron James moment? Chances are it is different than your best friend's. You might each have your own individual moment of greatness that you believe defines his career. The best part—you could both be right.

In Game 7 of the 2013 NBA Finals, the Miami Heat were looking to win back-to-back titles. They were at home, taking on the San Antonio Spurs to close out what had been a brutally hard-fought series. Game 7 would be no different.

It was back and forth all night, and with less than a minute left, the Heat held on to a two-point lead. James has already had a monster night, with 33 points and a dozen rebounds. But when his team needed him most, when the series and the title were on the line, the King delivered.

After Tim Duncan of the Spurs missed an easy game-tying basket, the Heat brought the ball up the court. The sold-out crowd on their feet at American Airlines Arena in Miami had little doubt who was going to get the ball. Off the time-out, James handled the inbounds pass, worked the perimeter, then appeared to be ready to drive to the hoop. Suddenly he pulled up, creating separation between himself and the defenders, and drained the jump shot to give the Heat a two-possession lead with less than 30 seconds to go.

The Spurs had one last-gasp effort: to make a foul on the other team and then hope to get the ball back. In the game, James was six-for-six from the free throw line, not great odds for the Spurs' strategy, yet they chose to send him back to the line with their season hanging in the balance. James coolly stepped up and buried both free throws, along with the Spurs' season. James had put the Heat on his back and carried them to their second NBA Championship title!

He finished the game with 37 points, 12 boards, four assists, and a pair of steals. He was a perfect five-for-five from three-point range and eight-for-eight from the free throw line. Dominant players—true superstars—always want the ball when the game is on the line. James is no different. When it matters most, King James takes control and delivers the clutch shots that propel his team to the title.

# FROM POVERTY TO RICHES

If the odds of a child growing up to play in the NBA are a million to one, then for LeBron James they were ten million to one. When James was born in Akron, Ohio, in 1984, his mother was just 16 years old and his father wasn't in the picture. James grew up poor.

His mother bounced around jobs, and that meant James lived his childhood on the move. He and his mom moved from apartment to apartment, packing up when they could no longer pay the rent. He slept on friends' couches, switched schools frequently, and struggled to fit in. One year he missed more than 100 days of school, playing video games alone. For young James, his days weren't spent visualizing a career in the NBA—they were spent surviving.

During those early years, basketball wasn't even a possibility. His sports interest began with football, a game he was introduced to when a coach saw him race some friends in a parking lot and recognized that his speed was special. At nine years old, James played running back for the East Dragons, an under-10 youth football team in Akron. His athletic gifts were immediately evident: his size and speed made him impossible to tackle.

When James did begin to play basketball, it began with a milk crate nailed to a telephone pole to form a crude basket. Who could have ever imagined that the couch-surfing poor kid from Akron shooting a ball through a milk crate would one day grow up to be an NBA superstar?

By middle school, LeBron was already dunking the basketball, and as a freshman at St. Vincent-St. Mary High

School, he was already receiving national attention from scouts and the media. James earned the hype. He led his team to a perfect 27–0 record as a freshman, winning the State Championship. Later, as a junior, James was featured on the cover of *Sports Illustrated*. It was a first in the history of the magazine. Under a picture of James clowning for the camera, the headline proclaimed him to be "the Chosen One."

But there would be no college for LeBron James when he left high school in 2003. The NBA now has a rule barring teams from drafting players straight from high school. This rule didn't exist in 2003. Thus, the Cleveland Cavaliers used the first overall selection in the 2003 NBA Draft to select St. Vincent-St. Mary forward LeBron James. The kid who grew up in poverty in Akron was now a millionaire in Cleveland.

# OCTOBER 29, 2003: THE DAY IT ALL BEGAN

After years of anticipation and more hype than had ever been afforded a high school athlete in any sport, LeBron James took the court on the road against the Sacramento Kings. The world watched and wondered how the teenager the media called The Chosen One would respond in his first regular season NBA game.

His first NBA touches offered some insight into the well-rounded player the Cavs had acquired. Less than two minutes into his first game, James went hard to the basket and pulled down a defensive rebound. He glided up the court before delivering a beautiful alley-oop pass, hitting Ricky Davis in stride for a slam dunk. James would finish his first professional game leading his team in points (25), assists (nine), and steals (four).

James later gave an interview during his rookie season where he explained how he handled his new life in the NBA. "There's no pressure for me, because I'm doing something I love to do, that's play the game of basketball," he said. His rookie campaign of 2003–04 was a continuous highlight reel. He posted seven games with 30 or more points and appeared in all 82 games for the Cavs. He was a runaway choice for the Rookie of the Year Award. And for the first time in a long time, fans in Cleveland had something to be excited about.

It took James two more seasons to lead the Cavaliers to their first playoff appearance. His first taste of the postseason came in a first-round matchup against the Washington Wizards. In the pivotal Game 5 of the series, James delivered a performance that still ranks among the best of his career. The Wizards had no answer for James from the opening tip-off. He drove the lane at will, using his size and strength to manhandle the Wizards' defenders. His outside game was on point as he time and again pulled up to shoot finesse jump shots over the outstretched arms of the defenders.

But James saved his best for last. Trailing 120–119 with just 3.6 seconds left in the game, James took the inbounds pass from Larry Hughes. Many players would have panicked and thrown up the quick shot. Not James. He deftly weaved through the defense and calmly laid the ball up and in for the game winner. The Cavaliers went on to win the series and the legacy of James in the postseason was born.

# G.O.A.T.

When he eventually walks away from the game, James' legacy will be a simple one in many fans' eyes: He will leave basketball as the greatest basketball player of all time. Sure, many will point to Michael Jordan's achievements in the natural counterargument to the "LeBron is the greatest" claim, but that's where the nuances of LeBron's career form his legacy and his place in history as the G.O.A.T. (Greatest of All Time).

Consider this: M. J. won six titles, but he did it with a single dynasty team. LeBron has shown the ability to win championships with multiple teams. LeBron has already topped M. J. in every major statistical category—including points, rebounds, assists, and blocks. He has more All-Star appearances and he even tops Jordan in Olympic medals, 3–2.

Fans will argue that Jordan stepped away from the game for four seasons in two separate retirements and, had he played, he would have the numbers to top LeBron. The fact that he has performed at the highest level for so many years, without a break, simply adds to King James' legacy. Straight from high school, he stepped into the NBA and transformed the league.

Off the court, James has strengthened his legacy through a variety of avenues. His philanthropy through the LeBron James Family Foundation includes founding an elementary school in his hometown of Akron to serve disadvantaged youth. Through his foundation, he also pledged to spend more than $41 million to pay for 1,100 Akron students to attend college for free. His charitable work off the court has earned him many accolades, including the NBA Citizenship Award.

James is also an accomplished businessman. He owns his own video production company, SpringHill Entertainment, and a sports media company called Uninterrupted. He is co-owner of dozens of businesses, including pizza franchises as well as sneaker and clothing stores. He even owns a stake in soccer club Liverpool F.C.! His estimated income in 2019 was $89 million, with almost two thirds of that cash coming from his business ventures and endorsements. Wealth doesn't make a legacy, but what a person does with that wealth certainly does, and James has chosen to use his fame and fortune to contribute millions of dollars to help young people excel, to create jobs, and to create generational security for his family.

Years from now, as historians reflect on the game of basketball, the legacy of LeBron James will be summed up in seven simple words: The greatest that ever played the game.

# CANDACE PARKER

## WNBA POWER FORWARD  3

| | |
|---|---|
| **BIRTH YEAR** | 1986 |
| **BIRTHPLACE** | ST. LOUIS, MISSOURI |
| **HEIGHT \| WEIGHT** | 6'4" \| 175 LBS |
| **YEARS ACTIVE** | 2013–PRESENT |

**TEAMS**

LOS ANGELES SPARKS, UMMC EKATERINBURG, GUANGDONG DOLPHINS, ISTANBUL FENERBAHÇE S.K.; XINJIANG TIANSHAN DEERS

WNBA Rookie of the Year, 2008

WNBA All-Star, 2011, 2013, 2014, 2017–2018

WNBA MVP, 2008, 2013

WNBA Finals MVP, 2016

WNBA Rebounding Leading, 2008, 2009

John R. Wooden Award, 2007, 2008

AP Female Athlete of the Year, 2008

🐦 @Candace_Parker

📷 @CandaceParker

## CAREER STATISTICS

(THROUGH THE 2018–2019 SEASON)

**315**
GAMES PLAYED

**1,230**
ASSISTS

**5,360**
POINTS

**518**
BLOCKS

**2,688**
REBOUNDS

61

# RISING ABOVE THE ADVERSITY

Everyone faces adversity, but when you are a professional female athlete trying to make a name for yourself in a sport dominated by coverage of the men's league, that adversity is only amplified. For Los Angeles Sparks superstar Candace Parker, that adversity has come in many forms during her career.

Basketball is a physical game, and players use the off-season to rest their bodies and minds, and to recover for the season ahead. For Parker, however, there is no off-season. Like all WNBA players, Parker's salary isn't what you might expect for a professional athlete. While top NBA players earn more than $30 million per season, the top WNBA salary is $127,000. To supplement her WNBA salary, Parker travels overseas, playing in Russia, Turkey, and China. Between her WNBA career, her overseas career, and two trips to the Olympics, Parker has never experienced a true off-season. Without that built-in off-season, WNBA players like Parker are prone to more injuries. Though she is only in her early thirties, her body has endured a double-digit number of surgeries and grueling rehabilitations just to stay on the court.

Off the court, Parker has faced the bad press that comes with being a six-foot-four female basketball player. She has faced the sexism, racism, and taunts that her professional team couldn't beat most high school boys' teams. Though she tries to channel all of that adversity to fuel her on the court, she isn't immune to the hurt, especially when it comes to issues of race.

"Racism has been an issue in our country for a very long time, but women's suffrage has been here an even longer time," she said during a WNBA roundtable discussion with some of the league's top players. "So, with that combination, being black *and* a woman, you know . . ." She doesn't bother to finish the sentence, because every woman at the table *does* know. Still, Parker is proud of her career and all that she has accomplished on the court. She is proud to be a role model for her daughter. And she is proud to have overcome so much, battled so hard, and still be standing on the top of the mountain.

"You know, there's obstacles in life, and it's about how you handle it," she said in an interview prior to the start of the 2016 season. "Sometimes it's not what happens, but rather your reaction to it."

# A ONE-HANDED, HISTORY-MAKING DUNK

First-round NCAA Tournament games don't often generate much national buzz. Such was the case in 2006, when the second-seeded Tennessee Lady Volunteers took on the 15th-seeded Army Black Knights in the opening round of the tournament. Tennessee was expected to easily top Army in the game, which they did 102–54. It was the game within that lopsided victory that made history.

Early in the first half, with the Lady Vols holding a two-point lead, Tennessee's Sidney Spencer grabbed a loose ball and tossed a long pass downcourt, leading

Parker. The freshman raced toward the basket with one defender trailing her. Parker drove to the hoop, leaped in the air, and delivered a one-handed dunk! It may have been only two points, but it was a historic basket as Parker became the first woman in the history of the NCAA Tournament to dunk the ball. Later, early in the second half with her team comfortably out in front by 31 points, Parker delivered her second dunk of the game.

Though Parker won the Slam Dunk contest at the McDonald's High School All-American Game in 2004, dunked in a high school game, and then set the NCAA Tournament record with her two dunks against Army in 2006, she prides herself on being a complete basketball player. She has resisted being too closely linked to her ability to dunk the basketball. Following her history-making effort against Army, Parker was quick to downplay the achievement. "I've only dunked in one game. I don't want that to be my identity," she said at the time. "I want to be known for an all-around game."

The reality is, in a sport where very few women dunk, Parker's ability to do so has earned her accolades. In more than 100 years, no woman had ever accomplished what Parker did that night in Cleveland. And in the 23-year history of the WNBA, only seven players have dunked in a game, including Parker. By the time she threw down her first WNBA dunk, the magnitude of the NCAA milestone had changed for Parker and she seemed more willing to embrace her role as a power player. "I was really excited to do it in front of the Los Angeles Sparks fans," she said in an interview following the game.

Parker sees herself as paving the way for future girls to follow in her footsteps the way she followed in those of Lisa Leslie, her Sparks teammate and the first WNBA player to dunk in league history. "Lisa was the first generation, I'm the next generation," she said. "Then there's gonna be somebody out here doing windmills, it's just a matter of time."

# INSPIRED BY HER BROTHERS

Candace Parker grew up in Naperville, Illinois, near Chicago. That meant, like nearly everyone she knew, she was a Chicago Bulls fan. It was the height of Michael Jordan's career and Parker was exposed to a lot of basketball growing up. In addition to watching Jordan, Scottie Pippen, and Dennis Rodman perform for the Bulls, Parker watched her older brothers Anthony and Marcus. Both were serious basketball players and Parker would often accompany them to the park with their dad, Larry, while they played.

Despite this early exposure and eventual love for the game, Parker didn't have any plans to play basketball herself. She was a soccer player as a youth. But as Parker was preparing to head to high school, things changed. Encouraged by her father and inspired by her brothers, she decided to take up basketball competitively. "I always wanted to do everything they did," she said of her brothers. "They're so much older than me, so we never really played against each other. I just really did everything they did and wanted to emulate their game."

With her height, natural athletic ability, and competitive nature, Parker soon excelled at basketball. At Naperville Central High School, Parker was an instant superstar. Her high school coach, Andrew Nussbaum, shared a story with *USA Today* in 2018 recounting the night Parker dunked the ball for the first time in a high school game. "She got it on the break, and you could tell that she was gonna try again," he said. "Then she just threw it down. It wasn't a home game, and there were a lot of people there, but I think everyone was just shocked. It was pretty incredible."

Nussbaum shared another side of Parker in that interview, one that speaks to her character. "She loved to fill the water cups for her teammates when she wasn't playing. She's probably the best high school girls player to ever play the game, and here she is doubling as the water girl," he said. "She also used to look at the scorebook to see who hadn't scored yet, so she could get them the ball."

After graduation, Parker parlayed her high school achievements into a scholarship to play Division 1 ball at the University of Tennessee under legendary coach Pat Summit. In college, Parker was a force for the Lady Vols, leading the team to back-to-back National Championships. Instead of playing in her senior season, Parker turned her sights toward the 2008 Summer Olympics in Beijing, China, followed by a career in professional basketball.

In April 2008, Parker was taken by the Los Angeles Sparks with the first overall pick in the WNBA draft. Four months later, she reached her other goal, winning the Gold Medal as part of Team USA.

# THE PROS AND A LONG-AWAITED TROPHY

Parker's WNBA career kicked off with a road game against the Phoenix Mercury, and the rookie was shining from the opening tip-off. All night she alternated between driving the lane and drawing fouls, to showing off her perimeter game with three-pointers, jumps shots, and several nifty left-handed baskets. She finished the first game of her career with a team high of 34 points as her Sparks topped the Mercury, 99–94. Parker finished her rookie campaign averaging 18.5 points per game and 9.5 boards. The 22-year-old became the first player in WNBA history to win both the Rookie of the Year Award and the league MVP Award in the same season.

Despite Parker's continued stellar performance, the Sparks fell short of the championship year after year. The team hadn't taken home a championship trophy since 2003. Finally, in 2016, the Sparks broke through. It was the first and only season of her career that Parker started every game. She led the Sparks to a 26–8 record in the regular season, but it was the postseason that mattered. Analysts felt like this was the best Sparks team of Parker's tenure. However, they didn't win their division, instead finishing second to the Minnesota Lynx and entering the postseason as the number two seed. Could Parker lead an upset and overcome their rivals for the title?

First, the Sparks had to get past the Chicago Sky. Parker made that look easy, leading her team in scoring in all three wins as the Sparks cast aside the Sky, 3–1. Parker averaged 26 points per game in her team's three wins.

From there it was the WNBA Finals and a meeting with the top-seeded Minnesota Lynx, their division rival led by Maya Moore. After a quiet first two games in the series, Parker exploded in Game 3 with 24 points, leading the Sparks to a crucial home win and a 2–1 series lead. The Lynx took Game 4, setting up a dramatic finale for the WNBA Championship.

With the season and the title on the line, Parker was money. She banged bodies hard on the boards, collecting 12 rebounds in the game along with scoring 28 points, none more important than her final basket. Trailing 74–73 with 23 seconds left in the road game, the Sparks needed a bucket. Parker delivered, grabbing a nifty feed from teammate Nneka Ogwumike and banking a shot off the glass for the lead. Two possessions later, the Sparks were the WNBA Champions and Parker was named the series MVP.

# A VOICE FOR GENDER EQUALITY

After a dozen years in her professional career, the two-time league MVP is still playing at a very high level. Critics make the argument that Parker won't be remembered among the game's elite players unless she adds at least one more championship to her resume. The great ones are typically measured by wins and losses, and Parker has only held the championship trophy a single time. Nonetheless, her fans will counter that basketball is a team sport and Parker can't win titles on her own.

Further, the record books will show that her performance has led to a Rookie of the Year Award, five All-Star Game appearances, and two league MVP awards, in 2008 and 2013. Then there are her off-season achievements. Parker has absolutely dominated overseas, capturing four consecutive Russian National League titles from 2011 to 2015.

Perhaps her legacy will be defined by the "what ifs" of her career. What if Parker hadn't endured seven knee surgeries? What if she hadn't dislocated her shoulder in 2010 during a game? Injuries are part of professional sports, but Parker seems to have had more than her fair share. What if she had been able to stay healthier—would there be more titles?

Time will tell how Parker's legacy is viewed on the court. But like many WNBA players, she will be remembered as much for her pioneering efforts off the court to advance the game of women's basketball. Players and fans of the WNBA have long been outspoken about the need for higher player salaries. Parker has been among those voices.

But there is another area where she has led a unique conversation for the game of basketball: gender equality. Parker is outspoken that there ought to be equality and a sense of oneness among professional basketball players on both sides of the gender line. (It is worth noting that Parker was married to former NBA player Shelden Williams, and her brother is former NBA player Anthony Parker.)

In a league where many of the players hold basketball camps and other events aimed at working with young girls, Parker pursues a different direction. Her basketball programs include boys *and* girls learning the game side by side. "I think it's just as important for guys and girls to understand that leaders can come in different shapes, sizes, backgrounds, whatever," Parker said in 2019. "And you can't just preach to girls, because that's not going to create change."

# HONORABLE MENTIONS
## POWER FORWARDS

### GIANNIS ANTETOKOUNMPO

The man they call "the Greek Freak" has put the Milwaukee Bucks back on the map as a legitimate NBA powerhouse. Giannis Antetokounmpo took an unusual route to the NBA. Born in Greece to Nigerian parents, Antetokounmpo didn't even begin playing basketball until he was a teenager. When he eventually joined a youth team in Greece, he walked four miles each way to practice and often slept in the gym afterward.

In 2013, Antetokounmpo became eligible for the NBA draft and the Milwaukee Bucks selected the 18-year-old as the 15th pick. Since then, he has improved every year in the league, posting remarkable numbers the last three seasons and earning three consecutive trips to the All-Star Game.

In 2019, he posted career highs with 30.5 points and 12.9 rebounds per game, capturing his first NBA MVP Award. His rise has coincided with the success of the Bucks. The team made the playoffs in each of Antetokounmpo's All-Star years, and although he hasn't delivered an NBA title to Milwaukee, most experts think it is only a matter of time.

# BLAKE GRIFFIN

Blake Griffin's career is a complicated arc. Drafted in 2009 by the Los Angeles Clippers with the first overall pick, Griffin missed his entire first season due to injury. He bounced back in 2010–11, capturing the Rookie of the Year Award and earning the first of five consecutive All-Star nods. Then the injury bug returned. Griffin missed big parts of the next three seasons battling foot, shoulder, and hand injuries. Despite posting strong numbers even during his injury-filled seasons, the Clippers had seen enough. In the 2017–18 season, the Clippers traded away their former top pick to the Detroit Pistons. But Griffin wasn't done.

In his first season as a Piston, the six-foot-nine, 250-pound man delivered a career high in points, averaging 24.5 in 75 games. He returned to his pre-injury form and, on October 23, delivered a performance reminiscent of his early years in Los Angeles. Taking on the Philadelphia 76ers at home, Griffin had a monster game. He poured in a career-high 50 points, scoring from all over the floor. But it was in overtime that Griffin delivered his best basketball.

With the Pistons trailing 132–130 with five seconds to go, Detroit was down to its last shot. Griffin took the inbounds pass, drove the lane, and laid in the basket to tie the game with 1.8 seconds on the clock! But he wasn't done. Griffin drew the foul on the play and stepped to the line with a chance to win the game. Griffin coolly knocked down the game winner, capping the best offensive night of his NBA career.

# TINA CHARLES

Over the last decade, Tina Charles has proven to be one of the most reliable and consistent players in the WNBA. Since being drafted by the Connecticut Sun in 2010, Charles has never missed any stretch of time due to injury. She has averaged more than 18 points and nearly 10 rebounds per game and has been named a perennial All-Star, making seven appearances in her 10 seasons.

In five trips to the postseason, Charles has been the player her teams have leaned on to deliver big games. Her deepest playoff run came in 2015 with the New York Liberty. Charles put up 122 points in the Liberty's two playoff series. The knock on Charles is that she has never led her team to a WNBA Championship title. But the 2012 WNBA MVP has dominated for a decade and the lack of championship rings doesn't diminish that. She holds the record for the fastest player to reach 50 career double-doubles, doing it in her first 75 WNBA games. She led the league in scoring in 2016 and she is an elite two-way player, having led the league in rebounding in four seasons. Charles is still in her prime, and whether the titles come or not, she is clearly an elite power forward in the WNBA.

# LEGENDARY GREAT
# POWER FORWARD

## *TIM DUNCAN*

Players are often judged by how they perform in clutch situations. With the game on the line, with one shot to win, do they deliver? In his prime, no player in the NBA was more clutch than San Antonio Spurs power forward Tim Duncan. An Internet search of Duncan's buzzer-beating clutch shots will keep you busy for a long time.

But Duncan was more than just a clutch player. He was as complete a basketball player as the game has seen. On offense, he delivered countless buzzer beaters and crucial baskets. He posted a career average of 19 points per game over 19 seasons. But the big man was equally skilled on the defensive side of the ball. His play earned him All-Defensive First Team honors eight times. And if players are ultimately measured by how much they win, Duncan delivered. When he retired in 2016, Duncan was only the third player in league history to win 1,000 games. His winning wasn't limited to the regular season, however. Duncan raised the NBA Championship trophy five times for the Spurs, while becoming the only player in the history of the NBA to win a title in three different decades.

Duncan played his entire 19-year career for the Spurs. During that time, he had only one head coach: Gregg Popovich. When Duncan announced his retirement, "Pop" reflected on the career of the greatest player he ever coached. "He's been the best teammate anybody could ever imagine," Popovich said. He also credited Duncan with his success as a coach, saying, "I wouldn't be standing here today if it wasn't for Tim Duncan."

In addition to his five championship rings, Duncan's trophy case is crowded with the accolades befitting one of the greatest players to ever step onto an NBA court. He was named MVP of three of the five Finals he won. Duncan was twice named league MVP, in 2002 and 2003, and he added 15 All-Star Games, including being named MVP of the 2000 contest, to his resume.

Still, with his incredible on-court accomplishments, Duncan is often overlooked when talking about the game's greatest players. One reason for this is that San Antonio is a small-sized market. Unlike big media markets like New York and Los Angeles, San Antonio is a relatively quiet city; Spurs players aren't household names for more casual fans. People who have never watched a single NBA game know who Kobe, Shaq, LeBron, and M. J. are. Their fame is evident in the fact they are all identified by a single name. But ask any of Duncan's former teammates or coaches who they would want to have the ball with the game on the line and they would all pick number 21. Longtime teammate Tony Parker credited Duncan with making everyone he played with better players, saying, "that's the true definition of a superstar."

Of the countless game-winners and clutch shots that Duncan made over his 19-year career, highlighting just one is an impossible task. But a case can be made for the events of New Year's Eve, 2014. The Spurs were hosting the New Orleans Pelicans, and with the game tied at 82, Pelicans star Anthony Davis grabbed a rebound and dunked the ball home, giving the Pelicans the lead. With just seven tenths of a second left on the clock, the game was seemingly over.

San Antonio took a time-out, allowing for the inbounds pass at the other end of the court. Scoring with less than one second is impossible ... unless you have Tim Duncan. Boris Diaw was ready to inbound the ball. Duncan broke for the basket and Diaw lobbed a perfect high pass. The big man leaped for the basket and tipped the ball to the hoop. It rolled around the rim and fell in just as the clock expired! The game was going into overtime. In OT, Duncan added three more points and the Spurs ended 2014 with a thrilling overtime win, 95–93.

# STEPHEN CURRY

| | |
|---|---|
| **BIRTH YEAR** | 1988 |
| **BIRTHPLACE** | AKRON, OHIO |
| **HEIGHT \| WEIGHT** | 6'2" \| 185 LBS |
| **YEARS ACTIVE** | 2009–PRESENT |
| **TEAMS** | GOLDEN STATE WARRIORS |

NBA MVP, 2015, 2016

NBA All-Star, 2014–2019

NBA Scoring Champion, 2016

AP Athlete of the Year, 2015

## CAREER STATISTICS

(THROUGH THE 2018–2019 SEASON)

**694**
GAMES PLAYED

**4,588**
ASSISTS

**16,315**
POINTS

**154**
BLOCKS

**3,132**
REBOUNDS

 @StephenCurry30

@StephenCurry30

# A UNANIMOUS MVP

One of Stephen Curry's most historic moments happened off the court. It was May 10, 2016, and the Golden State Warriors were in the middle of a playoff run, looking to repeat as NBA Champions. The Warriors were taking on the Portland Trail Blazers in the Western Conference Semifinals. The previous night, Curry had returned from a knee injury to lead the Warriors with 40 points as they downed the Trail Blazers 132–125 in overtime. They held a commanding 3–1 lead in the series. May 10 was a rest day as the teams traveled back to California for Game 6. But Curry didn't have the day off. The defending NBA Champion and defending league MVP had a press conference to attend.

Curry spent his day off collecting his second consecutive NBA MVP Award. He had been unstoppable on the court during the 2015–16 season. His 30.1 points per game were best in the league. He also led the league in steals, field goals, three-pointers, and free throw percentage. His 402 three-point shots set the NBA record. No player had ever made 400 in a season. Curry dominated from start to finish, leading the Warriors to a 73–9 record and the top seed in the playoffs. But what made winning this MVP Award so historic? Wilt Chamberlain, Magic Johnson, Bill Russell, Michael Jordan, LeBron James, and Larry Bird were among the players who had won back-to-back awards. Fourteen different players had won the award and the NBA title in the same season. What made this one so special?

For Curry, it was the overwhelming, unprecedented

dominance with which he won the award that made history. The NBA MVP was chosen by a panel of 130 sportswriters in the United States and Canada. Fans were also given the chance to vote for their MVP. In more than 60 seasons, no player had ever been a unanimous selection. That is, until Curry. The best three-point shooter in league history earned the nod from all 130 sportswriters and the fans, earning a place in history as the only unanimous MVP in the history of the award.

Curry celebrated the moment by returning to the court the next night and knocking the Trail Blazers out of the playoffs. Though his Warriors would eventually fall to LeBron and the Cavaliers 4–3 in the NBA Finals, Curry's 2015–16 season is still looked back on by many as the most dominant offensive season in basketball history.

# CURRY THE MAGICIAN

Steph Curry was having a career night on the road against the Oklahoma City Thunder in 2016. After trailing by 11 points at the half, Curry led the charge as the Warriors fought back. The Thunder were playing strong in front of the home crowd and with only minutes left in the game they held a seven-point lead. As Curry brought the ball up the court, he was looking for a teammate to dish to. He quickly pulled up from long distance and launched a three-pointer, banking it in to cut the lead to four. A minute later, with his team trailing by five, Curry duplicated the long-range three-pointer, knocking it down to bring the

Warriors within two points. Golden State completed the comeback and tied the game at 103–103 to force overtime.

Curry was on a scorching pace from the three-point line, hitting 11 of his first 15 shots from beyond the arc. In overtime, he took over. Curry scored his team's first seven points in the extra frame and knocked down 12 of the Warriors' 18 overtime points, assisting on the other two field goals.

Despite his dominance and the fact that Thunder superstar (and future teammate) Kevin Durant had fouled out early in OT, the game was tied 118–118 with less than 30 seconds to go. After the Thunder failed to score on the next possession, Golden State's Andre Iguodala grabbed the rebound. The stage was set for Curry magic ... and he didn't disappoint.

Curry took the pass from Iguodala and pushed it up the court. As the clock wound down, Warriors coach Steve Kerr elected not to use his final time-out. He was putting the game in his superstar's hands. Curry crossed half-court, dribbled once, and launched a long three-pointer. With six-tenths of a second left, the ball banked in and the Warriors won the game.

In a game where Curry set the new NBA record for most three-pointers made in a season, he had saved the most important one for the final second of the game!

# SMALL, BUT WITH A GOLDEN TOUCH

Wardell Stephen Curry II is the second greatest basketball player ever born in Akron, Ohio, behind only the King, LeBron James. Curry was born March 14, 1988, while his dad, Dell Curry, was a member of the Cleveland Cavaliers. Steph Curry grew up around the game, and with a father who played pro ball and a mom who was a collegiate volleyball player, Curry and his younger brother, Seth, were destined to be athletes. The boys grew up on NBA courts, shooting around with Dell and his teammates. "I remember every game I went to," Curry said in a 2015 interview. "My dad was always a great role model for me."

Curry may have earned his golden touch from the three-point line from watching his dad. Dell knocked down more than 1,200 three-point shots during his career. Steph, known for his quick release when he gets the ball in his hands, also got that from the man he calls "pop."

In a 2009 conversation with Steph, Dell recounts, "I wasn't quick, and I couldn't jump, so I had to get it off the best way I could, the fastest way I could," explaining where his quick-release style came from. Growing up, Curry studied his dad and learned the game, whether it was at his father's team practices or at home in the family's driveway.

His father's NBA career meant the Currys moved around a bit. Steph was born in Ohio, raised in North Carolina, spent time in Toronto, and returned to Charlotte once Dell retired. Through it all, basketball was the common denominator. Still, even with his father as his mentor, early on it looked like Steph might not have the body for the game.

In his high school freshman season at Charlotte Christian School, Curry stood only five feet seven and weighed just 130 pounds. (He was so small that he couldn't wear number 30, his dad's NBA number. The team's number 30 jersey only came in XL and was way too big for Curry, so he had to settle on number 20.) Because of his size, he didn't even try out for the varsity squad, opting to play junior varsity instead. In 2015, he called that decision a mistake. "One of my only regrets is not trying out [for varsity] that year," he said. "That taught me to go for it. To not let what people might tell you—no matter how short or skinny you might be—deter you from getting where you want to go."

But as Curry grew, so too did his basketball skills. After a lone season playing JV, Curry led the varsity squad at Charlotte Christian for the next three seasons, winning three state championships and parlaying his success into a scholarship offer to play locally at Davidson College in North Carolina.

Curry dominated at Davidson, starting all three years and leaving the school as its all-time leading scorer. By 2009, the kid who was too small to make his high school varsity team was ready to go pro.

# A SLOW BUT STEADY START

His father, Dell, was a first-round draft pick of the Utah Jazz in the 1986 NBA Draft. Could Steph follow in his dad's footsteps? Following his decision to declare for the 2009 NBA Draft, some still said that Curry was too small to succeed in the NBA. His ball handling and shooting were unquestioned, but would his body be able to hold up to the grind and the physical nature of the NBA game? The Golden State Warriors thought so. They used the seventh pick in the first round of the 2009 Draft to make Curry a Warrior.

While some players may begin their careers unhappy with the team that drafted them, Curry was excited to be a Warrior from the start. At his opening press conference, he talked about the thrill it was to take his game to the professional level. "I see Golden State as a great fit for the way I play, and the direction this team is going." Seated alongside Warriors general manager Larry Riley at that opening press conference, Curry had no way of knowing that he was the critical piece in what was to become the next great NBA dynasty.

After Curry's introduction to the league, the Warriors continued to struggle, missing the playoffs in each of his first three seasons. Curry's transition to the NBA wasn't as immediately dominant as, say, LeBron's. He would be four seasons in before the future Hall of Famer would average more than 20 points in a season. Instead, his adaptation to the pro game was slow and steady. In the 2011–12 campaign, for instance, he missed more than 50 games due to injury. The ankle problems Curry suffered early in his career were thought for a time to be potentially career-ending. Luckily, the medical staff was able to get Curry healthy and back on the court. Since then, his ankle has held up fine and he has gone on to become arguably the best shooter in the NBA.

"It was a little rough my first few years, but I loved playing at Oracle. . . . [Y]ou go around the league and you see different arenas, that's somewhere you want to play 41-plus games in every night," he said in a 2015 interview.

With his health at the best it had been, Curry took his game to the next level in the 2012–13 season. Curry averaged almost 23 points per game, and the Warriors broke through with their first playoff appearance in six years. Though they were knocked out by the Denver Nuggets in the first round of the playoffs, Golden State had arrived. They have appeared in the playoffs every year since then and have done pretty well, appearing in five straight NBA Finals and winning three titles.

## SAVING A FRANCHISE

When considering Steph Curry, it would be easy to focus solely on his dominance from behind the three-point arc. His critics will want to dismiss his NBA Championship titles, pointing out that he was part of arguably one of the most unstoppable dynasties ever built in any sport. They will compare his overall numbers to LeBron, M. J., and others, and argue he was a great player, but not the best. But a player's legacy is more than just the number of titles won or the number of individual records held.

Curry will be remembered as a player who saved a franchise. A player who helped reignite the passion for basketball for an entire city. Before the Warriors drafted Curry in the first round of the 2009 NBA Draft, the franchise had missed the playoffs 14 out of its previous 15 seasons. The team was bad, the fan base was disinterested, and the future looked grim. In his 10 years with Golden State, Curry has led the Warriors to the playoffs seven consecutive times. The team appeared in five straight NBA Finals, collecting three NBA titles.

Beyond the titles, Curry brings a level of excitement to every game. Curry is so electric shooting three-pointers that even non-fans tune in to watch him in action. His ability to make a basket from anywhere on the court anytime in the game makes every second of Warriors' basketball must-watch television.

In 2019, Curry was asked about his legacy. "When everyone asks me about legacy, I don't know, I don't want to ruin the moment," he said on the *Today* show. In the humble fashion he's known for, the Warriors leader dismissed any talk of being one of the all-time greats. "I feel like the way I got here was by keeping my head down and grinding," he said. "I'm not going to switch that up."

When he finally decides to leave the game behind, Steph Curry will be a lock for the Hall of Fame. He will be the greatest player in Golden State's history. And he will be remembered as a player who played the game hard and always seemed to have fun doing it.

# SUE BIRD

## WNBA POINT GUARD

**10**

| | |
|---|---|
| **BIRTH YEAR** | 1980 |
| **BIRTHPLACE** | SYOSSET, NEW YORK |
| **HEIGHT \| WEIGHT** | 5'9" \| 150 LBS |
| **YEARS ACTIVE** | 2002–PRESENT |
| **TEAMS** | SEATTLE STORM |

WNBA All-Star, 2002, 2003, 2005–2007, 2009, 2011, 2014, 2015, 2017, 2018

WNBA Top 15 Players All-Time

WNBA All-Decade Team

WNBA Champion, 2004, 2010, 2018

Russian National League Champion, 2007, 2008, 2012–14

NCAA Champion, 2000, 2002
Olympic Gold Medalist

 @S10Bird

 @SBird10

## CAREER STATISTICS

(THROUGH THE 2019 SEASON)

**508**
GAMES PLAYED

**2,831**
ASSISTS

**6,154**
POINTS

**62**
BLOCKS

**1,311**
REBOUNDS

# BIRD AT THE BUZZER

In the 2001 Big East Championship, the UConn Huskies faced off against the Notre Dame Fighting Irish in a showcase game that pitted two powerhouse women's basketball schools against each other. After a back-and-forth battle, with just 38 seconds left in the game, UConn held a 76–75 lead and had possession. Sue Bird, then a junior at UConn, worked the ball around the perimeter. Bird's job was to chew up time on the clock, but she committed a costly turnover, giving Notre Dame possession with 16 seconds to go. Notre Dame center Ruth Riley drove to the basket with a chance to win the game but drew a hard foul. Riley missed the first free throw, then sank the second to tie the game at 76 with 5.1 seconds to go. The Huskies had five seconds to drive the length of the court and make the game-winner.

Bird took the inbounds pass and it was clear she had no plans to play for overtime. She was looking for redemption for her earlier mistake. Bird sprinted up the court, crossing half-court and driving to her left. She crossed over, drove into the paint, and pulled up for the game-winning jump shot. The ball rattled off the front of the rim and fell in! Her teammates mobbed Bird on the court to celebrate their 2001 Big East title.

Notre Dame would have a chance to avenge the loss, however, when the two teams met later in the 2001 Final Four. Bird and the Huskies were the defending National Champions and, with a 12-point lead at the half, looked to be on their way to repeating as champions. But the Irish had revenge on their minds and came out of the locker room on fire. They quickly erased the 12-point deficit and went on to an easy 15-point win. UConn was sent home; Notre Dame went on to win the National title.

Two decades later, the game and Bird's shot are remembered as one of the biggest games and biggest moments in women's college basketball history. The game was even immortalized in a book coauthored by longtime NBA and WNBA analyst Doris Burke, *Bird at the Buzzer*. For Bird, with all of her on-court accomplishments—from WNBA Championship titles to Olympic Gold Medals—"the shot" is still the play she will forever be remembered for and is most often asked about.

# EXCELLENCE UNDER PRESSURE

At the end of the 2010 season, more than 15,000 screaming fans found themselves on their feet as the Seattle Storm faced the biggest moment of the WNBA season. It was Game 1 of the Finals and Seattle was Hosting the Atlanta Dream. The game was knotted at 77–77, with the clock winding down. The Storm had one last chance to end the game in regulation, and they drew up a play that would put the ball in the hands of Sue Bird to win it.

During the regular season, Bird was only third on the team in scoring. Her 11.1 points per game trailed teammates Lauren Jackson (20.5) and Swin Cash (13.8). Jackson had the hot hand in Game 1, dropping 26 points to lead all scorers. While Bird played a strong game, her stat line read just 12 points scored. But when the game was on the line, Storm coach Brian Agler wanted Bird taking the final shot.

Bird brought the ball to the top of the key as the clock ran under five seconds. She crossed over her dribble, pulled up, and took an uncontested jumper from the top of the key. Bird sank the pressure-packed bucket with just 2.6 seconds left to give the Storm the Game 1 win!

After the win, Bird was asked why she seemed to perform so well in those high-pressure situations. "You get confidence, the more you do things, and the more you are successful," she said in the postgame press conference. "At this point in my career, it's something I enjoy, those situations are fun."

The game-winning shot gave Seattle all of the momentum in the best of five series. Two nights later they won 87–84, finishing an undefeated season at home and posting a perfect 21–0 record. After shutting down the Dream in Atlanta to complete the series sweep, Bird collected her second WNBA Championship title. She was asked after the game what it meant to her. "It's been a long time since 2004 [the Storm's last title] and to get back, to win, to go undefeated in the playoffs and have the best record, I couldn't be happier."

# MAKING THE RIGHT CHOICES EARLY ON

Sue Bird was born in Syosset, New York, in 1980 and is the youngest of two children born to Herschel, a doctor, and Nancy, a nurse. Bird credits her older sister, Jen, with getting her interested in playing basketball when she was seven years old. "I looked up to Jen," Bird said in an interview for UConn Hoop Legends' website. "I wanted to do whatever Jen did."

Bird didn't limit herself to just basketball, however. She excelled at soccer, tennis, and track as well. Still, it was clear to those around her that Bird had what it takes to be special on the basketball court. After two years of playing varsity basketball at Syosset High School, Bird's parents made the decision to move their daughter to a private school to focus on her basketball game. Christ the King Regional High School had a reputation for propelling players to the pros. NBA stars Lamar Odom and Jayson Williams, as well as WNBA stars Tina Charles and Chamique Holdsclaw all graduated from the school.

The decision to transfer proved to be the right one for Bird. She excelled at Christ the King, with the team going undefeated at 27–0 in her first season and winning the New York State Championship. She managed to top that during her senior season in 1997–98. The Royals once again went undefeated. Bird averaged more than 16 points, seven rebounds, and eight steals per game. The team captured its second state championship and Bird was named New York State Player of the Year.

Bird's play drew the interest of scouts from across the country. She had offers to play at some of the best schools in the nation, including the University of Connecticut and Stanford University. In the end, Bird says she liked the idea of staying close to home, so she chose to become a UConn Husky.

Like the decision to transfer to Christ the King, Bird's choice of UConn again proved to be the right one. She joined one of the most prestigious programs in women's college basketball. Over the next four years, she would be an integral part of the Huskies' success—UConn went an incredible 136–9. She won two National Championships, including capping off an undefeated senior season by winning her second crown.

"When we won the national championship, it was just a lot of emotion, a lot of feeling," Bird said in an interview for WNBA.com. "It was my four-year career in college coming down to this one moment where we go undefeated, win a national championship, and we're on top. That was just a great feeling." It was also the perfect way to end her college career and prepare for life in the pros.

# STATS DON'T TELL THE STORY WITH BIRD

In 2000 and 2001, the Seattle Storm had a combined record of 16–48. They won just 10 games in 2001, earning the top pick in the 2002 WNBA Draft. The team used that pick to select Sue Bird. Bird was one of four UConn Huskies selected in the top 10 of the draft. Her teammates Swin Cash (number two), Asjha Jones (number four), and Tamika Williams (number six) joined her at the draft podium. For Bird, it was the culmination of years of hard work. Two high schools and a four-year college career had netted Bird four titles, and now it had earned her the distinction of being the number one pick in the WNBA draft.

Six weeks later, Bird took the court for her first professional game. The Storm were hosting the New York Liberty, and Bird was starting at guard. The rookie wasted no time establishing herself as worthy of the top pick. She led all scorers in the game with 18 points and added seven rebounds and a pair of assists. The Storm lost Bird's first game, 78–61, but with her strong play they won 17 games that year—more than the previous two seasons combined.

Bird built on her impressive rookie season, in which she earned the first of 11 All-Star Game appearances, by coming back with a strong sophomore campaign in 2003. Overall, Bird's pro career is defined by winning, even while her numbers have never been eye-popping. In 18 seasons in Seattle, Bird has only led the team in scoring twice. Her 12.1 points per game average might not scare anyone, but those who have played with her and against her know that Bird can't be defined by statistics. She was a key cog in the Storm's three WNBA Championships (2004, 2010, and 2018). She has also built a solid career playing overseas during the WNBA off-season.

Though she missed the entire 2019 season after suffering a knee injury, Bird has been incredibly reliable throughout her career. She is the all-time leader in games played in WNBA history (508) and assists (2,831). Bird is also in the top 10 in career points scored.

# A LEGACY OF GRACE UNDER PRESSURE

Though she is one of the oldest players in the WNBA, Sue Bird hasn't shown any signs of being ready to quit. Like many of the trailblazing stars of the WNBA, her legacy will be two-part.

On the court, Bird has made her case for being one of the best of all time. The 11-time All-Star has won at every level. She collected a pair of state championships at Christ the King High School, then followed up with two NCAA Championships as a member of the UConn Huskies. Bird next collected three titles as the leader of the Seattle Storm. If that isn't enough, she owns four Olympic Gold Medals earned as a member of Team USA.

Bird will also be remembered for her grace under pressure. August 5, 2011 is a day that Storm fans will remember for a long time to come. The visiting Connecticut Sun held a one-point lead with three seconds left in the game. Storm guard Katie Smith was set to inbound the ball. She looked for Bird and found her at the top of the key. Without panicking, Bird dribbled once and pulled up for the three-pointer. She drained the shot as time expired, giving the Storm the 81–79 win! In the most dire moments, Bird has a knack for delivering the big play.

Off the court, Bird has an equally strong presence. She has joined the fight for pay equality for WNBA players. She has spent a decade playing overseas in the off-season, something she says is necessary due to the relatively low salaries she and her teammates earn. "Look, we're not over here saying we should be paid the same as the men," Bird said in a 2019 interview with *Ms.* magazine. "We understand that this is a business and that their revenue is insane compared to ours, but there is a bias that exists." She continues to work tirelessly to educate the public about that bias.

Bird has also become a public figure in the fight for gay rights. In 2019, she and her girlfriend, soccer star Megan Rapinoe, shared the cover of *ESPN the Magazine*'s annual Body Issue. It was the first time a same-sex couple had graced the cover of the popular magazine. Bird said she hopes the couple has paved the way for others to follow. "I think having a gay couple on [the cover], hopefully it just becomes the norm," she said in a 2019 interview with ESPN. "You want it to just be, 'Oh, another couple is on there.' You know, I think for us to be on it is the first step in that direction." For Bird, it is another feather in her cap as she builds a legacy that reaches beyond the basketball court.

# HONORABLE MENTIONS
## POINT GUARDS

### *RUSSELL WESTBROOK*

Westbrook has benefitted from playing alongside Kevin Durant and James Harden for much of his career. But although he may have taken a back seat to the higher-profile players on his teams, Westbrook has consistently delivered superstar-level stats over the last decade. The eight-time All-Star and two-time scoring champion was a steady force for the Oklahoma City Thunder from 2008 to 2019, before being surprisingly traded to the Houston Rockets.

His biggest season was 2016–17, when Westbrook became only the second player in NBA history to average a triple-double for the season. He also collected the League MVP Award that year. The knock on Westbrook is his lack of championship titles. His former teammate Durant didn't win a title until he left OKC. Many believe that, having been reunited with Harden in Houston, it is only a matter of time before Westbrook holds the NBA Championship trophy.

# KYRIE IRVING

Despite the turmoil that seems to follow him around, Irving has remained a productive—even dominant, at times—point guard over his career. His resume includes six All-Star Game appearances (he was named MVP of the 2014 game), a Rookie of the Year Award in 2012, and the ring he collected with LeBron in Cleveland in 2016. His career-long 22 points per game is solid, though he has yet to play a full 82-game slate since entering the NBA.

No one questions Kyrie Irving's talent on the basketball court. Yet it's some of the baggage the Nets' newest superstar carries with him that relegates him to an honorable mention. Paired with LeBron in Cleveland, Irving later forced his way out of town in a trade to the Boston Celtics. Soon he wore out his welcome in Boston and headed to Brooklyn, joining Kevin Durant on the Nets.

Irving lit up his debut with the Nets, setting an NBA record for the most points scored in a debut (50). If he can ease his off-court drama and continue to post numbers like that, he will soon silence his critics.

# COURTNEY VANDERSLOOT

Basketball is a game that can breed selfishness. Players are judged by points scored, game-winning shots, and how many individual awards they win. That's what makes the career of Chicago Sky point guard Courtney Vandersloot all the more impressive.

Vandersloot has led the WNBA in assists in four of her first nine seasons with the Sky. She is the ultimate team player, setting the table for her teammates to score. In 2018, Vandersloot set the WNBA single season record for assists when she delivered 258. She quickly broke her own record in 2019, dropping 300 assists in the regular season and another 23 in two postseason contests. In a book filled with scoring machines, Courtney Vandersloot is the selfless teammate that makes the Chicago Sky's offense run.

# LEGENDARY GREAT
# POINT GUARD

## MAGIC JOHNSON

The Lakers–Celtics rivalry of the 1980s is arguably the most renowned in the history of professional sports. Magic Johnson, Kareem Abdul-Jabbar, and James Worthy squaring off against Larry Bird, Robert Parrish, and Kevin McHale made for some incredibly exciting games. The two teams won a combined eight titles in the '80s and, thanks in large part to the dominant play of Earvin "Magic" Johnson, the Lakers collected five of those rings.

Magic's stardom began long before the Lakers made him the first overall pick in the 1979 NBA Draft. He capped off his college career at Michigan State by leading the Spartans to the NCAA Championship, where he poured in 24 points to lead all scorers in route to winning the tournament MVP. His arrival in Los Angeles began the dynasty run of the Lakers.

On the court, Johnson was arguably the most commanding point guard of his era. As a rookie, he led the Lakers to an NBA Championship. His performance in Game 6 against the Eastern Conference Champion Philadelphia 76ers is legendary. Against Dr. J and the 76ers, Magic put up a stat line of 42 points, 15 rebounds, and seven assists, playing a game-high 47 minutes. The Lakers knocked off the 76ers on their own court, 123–107, to win Magic's first title and his first Finals MVP Award.

At 20 years old, Johnson had already won a High School State Championship, an NCAA Championship, and an NBA Championship. And he was just getting warmed up. He would lead the Lakers to eight more appearances in the NBA Finals over his career, winning four more titles.

If you were only given one season to capture the greatness of Johnson's career, 1986–87 would be the year to choose. A case could be made that it was the best individual season in NBA history. Let's start with the pure stats: Johnson had career highs in games played (80) and points per game (23.9) and he led the league in assists (12.2). He was named to the All-Star Team for the sixth consecutive season, he earned All-NBA First Team honors, and he was named league MVP.

But Magic's greatness went deeper than individual statistics. What made him so special was his ability to make his teammates better and to win. He led the 1986–87 Lakers to a regular season record of 65–17, capturing the Pacific Division title. He then dominated in the playoffs as the Lakers went 11–1, defeating the Nuggets, Warriors, and Supersonics on the way to the NBA Finals and a matchup with the Celtics. For Johnson, it was showtime.

In a critical Game 1 win at home, Magic poured in 29 points. He went on to average 21 points and 12 rebounds per game, but it was the closing seconds of Game 4 that fans remember best. The Lakers trailed 106–105 with two seconds left. The Lakers inbounded to Johnson, and he looked to dish the ball off. The Celtics were playing tight and, with no other options, Johnson glided toward the paint and laid up a finger-roll hook shot. He knocked it down for the game-winner!

The crowd at the Boston Garden was stunned. The Lakers took the game 107–106 and won the series 4–2. Johnson collected his fourth ring and his third NBA Finals MVP Award. In eight years, he had transformed the Lakers into the most powerful dynasty in basketball.

# JAMES HARDEN

## NBA SHOOTING GUARD 13

| | |
|---|---|
| **BIRTH YEAR** | 1989 |
| **BIRTHPLACE** | LOS ANGELES, CALIFORNIA |
| **HEIGHT \| WEIGHT** | 6'5" \| 220 LBS |
| **YEARS ACTIVE** | 2009–PRESENT |
| **TEAMS** | OKLAHOMA CITY THUNDER, HOUSTON ROCKETS |

NBA MVP, 2018

All-Star, 2013–19

All-NBA First Team, 2014, 2015, 2017–19

NBA Sixth Man of the Year, 2012

 @BrittneyGriner

 @BrittneyYevetteGriner

## CAREER STATISTICS

(THROUGH THE 2018–2019 SEASON)

**765**
GAMES PLAYED

**4,743**
ASSISTS

**18,727**
POINTS

**383**
BLOCKS

**4,000**
REBOUNDS

# IN ATTACK MODE

The San Antonio Spurs came to Houston on March 22, 2019, to take on their cross-state rivals, the Houston Rockets. The Spurs' starting lineup posted 71 points in the game—solid numbers on any night. Unless, of course, you run into a red-hot James Harden, who matched his career-high by dropping 61 on the visitors to lead a 111–105 win.

Harden was hot from the opening tip-off and never took his foot off the gas. He dropped 27 points in the opening quarter alone. The Spurs had no answer for the big man. If they left him open on the perimeter, he killed them with three-pointers, dropping nine in the game, including draining five in the first half. If they played the man they call "the Beard" tight, he drove around his defenders and was relentless in the paint, scoring at will. When San Antonio contested Harden and he drew fouls, he was money at the line, adding 14 points from the charity stripe.

At times, Harden was so wide open on his shots that it appeared the Spurs had almost given up covering him. In reality, he was simply too much for the defense, as he poured in more than half of his team's points. After the game, Harden talked about his big night. "You've gotta be locked in," Harden said, describing what it takes to have a huge offensive night. "You've gotta have that mindset to where you're just in attack mode every play and that's what I was in tonight."

This was Harden's second 61-point game of the season. He had equaled the feat back in January on the road against the New York Knicks. In that game, Harden knocked down a handful of three-pointers, shot 22 from the free throw line, and when the game was tight in the fourth quarter, he poured in 12 points to seal the win. The Rockets were playing shorthanded, with several players out nursing injuries. A thin bench meant extended playing time for Harden, and with more pressure to carry the team, he responded. "We're limited guys, so whatever I have to do to try to win games, I'll do it, and coach knows that," he said following the win.

# HARDEN LAUNCHES A RAINBOW BALL

James Harden was having another monster offensive night for the Rockets in 2019. In the game, the Beard had scored 33 points on the road against the defending NBA Champion Golden State Warriors. Harden had buried seven three-pointers and led all scorers for the game. Still, the Warriors, led by Steph Curry with 35 points, tied the game at 119–119 and forced it into overtime. Facing off against the Warriors front three of Curry, Kevin Durant, and Klay Thompson, would the Rockets be able to steal a road win in OT?

A seesaw battle in overtime saw each team put up 13 points, and with 33 seconds left in the first overtime period the game was tied up at 132 each. The Warriors were driving, but Kevin Durant lost the ball. As it went out of bounds, Durant dove, swatting the ball back into play and saving the possession. The ball kicked out to Curry, who took two dribbles and buried a jumper to give the Warriors the lead, 134–132. After a loose ball out of bounds, the Rockets prepared to inbound the ball with 5.5 seconds on the clock. Gerald Green was inbounding for Houston and he was looking at Harden all the way. He found him deep, and Harden took the pass and tried to work free for a shot.

Klay Thompson was blanketing Harden on defense and, as the clock wound down, Draymond Green released from his man to set the double-team. As Harden went high in the air, extending over the double coverage, he launched a rainbow ball over both Warriors. The shot rattled in with one second on the clock, and the Rockets escaped Oakland with a huge road win thanks to the heroics of Harden.

Harden finished with a game-high 44 points, including 11 in the overtime frame. After the game, Harden was asked what it takes to deliver in those clutch moments. "[It takes] the work," Harden said. "Yesterday I was in that same spot [in practice] shooting that same shot, so I had confidence it was going to go in." The Warriors would have the last laugh when they met the Rockets again in the Western Conference Semifinals, easily besting Harden and company in six games and winning the series on Houston's home court.

# A WAY OUT OF COMPTON

Imagine stepping into the batter's box and seeing James Harden staring in at you from the pitcher's mound, ready to deliver a fastball with the same focus as when he drains jumpers for the Houston Rockets. That might sound like a crazy vision, but growing up in Compton, California, Harden began his athletic career on the diamond, not the hardcourt.

In a 2017 interview, Harden's mom, Monja Willis, talked about the importance of sports in the lives of the future NBA star and his older brother when they were kids. "By keeping them active in sports, that kept them out of gangs," she explained. "Anybody can come in and try to take advantage of them. That's why I focused on sports for them. They ended up loving it." In that same interview, Harden was asked about his youth career as a left-handed pitcher and first baseman. "I was a little Randy Johnson," he said, channeling the Hall of Fame pitcher and World Series champion.

After a failed attempt at basketball (his mom says he was too young to manage the fundamentals of the game), Harden's mom encouraged him to try baseball. Harden returned to the basketball court at age 10. Soon, he was playing year-round, whether in a local league or at home on a hoop nailed to the garage.

As a child, Harden battled asthma, a big challenge for a basketball player—the game demands a lot of cardio endurance. Sports helped the young Harden get in better shape and gradually he got his asthma under control.

By the time he reached high school, Harden was fixated on basketball. He would leave his house early most mornings, arriving at his school by 7:00 a.m. so he could work out in the gym before class. It is a work ethic that Harden maintains today as an established NBA superstar.

Those around him, including his mom, began to sense Harden might have what it takes to be something special on the basketball court. "I saw potential then," his mom told The Athletic website in a 2017 interview. "I didn't really like basketball or like sports, period. But I knew my kids had to do something to keep their mind busy." For Harden, sports, and basketball in particular, were a ticket off the tough streets of Compton and a way to steer clear of the gangs that drew in so many young men. Basketball was his road out.

After winning back-to-back state titles while at Artesia High School in Lakewood, California, and adding a Las Vegas Adidas Super 64 Championship in 2006, Harden was recruited to play basketball for Arizona State University. His career as a Sun Devil was short. After two seasons, during which he earned All-American honors and was named Pac-10 Player of the Year in 2009, Harden was ready to take the next step in his basketball journey. The kid from the mean streets of Compton was ready for the NBA.

# THE BENCH PLAYER TURNS INTO A STAR

"With the third pick in the 2009 NBA Draft, the Oklahoma City Thunder select James Harden of Arizona State University." With those words on June 25, 2009, NBA Commissioner David Stern made it official—James Harden was a professional basketball player!

But even on draft night the young James Harden wasn't lacking confidence in his game. "I don't think I need to prove anything," he said when asked about those who doubted the Thunder's decision to draft him so high. "I just need to go in there, work hard, and try my best to earn a spot on that team."

Unlike many high draft picks who are thrust into the starting lineup immediately, Harden began his career as a bench player. He didn't start a single game in his rookie season of 2009–10. In fact, the future league scoring champion only started seven games in three seasons in Oklahoma. Still, his game developed and improved, and even as a role player, Harden averaged 16.8 points per game in 2011–12. His strong play off the bench earned him the NBA Sixth Man Award. It also earned him an opportunity to move into a starting role—just not with the Thunder. On October 27, 2012, the Thunder announced they had traded Harden to the Houston Rockets. In Houston, Harden would sign an $80 million contract and become a starter for the first time in his NBA career.

The three-year bench player started 78 games in his first season in Houston, averaging an impressive 25.8 points per game. He also greatly improved on the dismal playoff performances that had become a sore spot in OKC. Harden seemed to disappear when the postseason arrived for the Thunder. In Houston, at least by the numbers, he delivered, averaging more than 26 points per game in his first postseason as a Rocket. Still, he had struggles in clutch moments.

Seven years into his tenure in Houston, Harden has developed into a premier shooter and one of the biggest offensive threats in the league. He has been named to the All-Star Game in all seven of his seasons in Houston and won the scoring title in back-to-back seasons.

But it was 2018 when it all came together. Harden broke the 30-point-per-game barrier for the first time in his career, averaging 30.2 for the season. He added nearly nine assists per game and led the Rockets to the Western Conference Finals. Though they came up short, losing the series 4–3 to the eventual NBA Champion Golden State Warriors, Harden ended the season with his first NBA MVP Award.

# A PLAYER WITH A COMPLEX LEGACY

Early in his career with Oklahoma City and early in his time in Houston, Harden developed a reputation as a player who couldn't deliver in the playoffs. Sure, his final stats in a game might look good, but in clutch moments in the fourth quarter when the team looked to Harden to lock it down, he missed with alarming frequency.

In 2015, Harden's Rockets were taking on the Golden State Warriors in the Western Conference Finals. With the Warriors leading the Series 3–1, Game 5 was do-or-die for the Rockets. When they needed him most, Harden delivered a record-breaking night—the kind of record you don't want to break. Harden turned the ball over 13 times, an NBA record, as the Warriors cruised to a 104–90 win to advance to the NBA Finals.

Until Harden wins an NBA Championship title, his legacy will reflect a great player who can't deliver when the spotlight is the brightest. The All-Star nods are great and the scoring titles are impressive, but a player labeled as selfish, who comes up empty in the playoffs, will likely be remembered as much for what he failed to accomplish as for what he achieved.

How James Harden will be remembered and the impact he will leave on the game are still being decided. Meanwhile, the Beard is still busy overpowering the NBA. One thing is certain: Harden's ultimate legacy will be a complex one. He will be remembered as one of the most feared offensive weapons in his era. The man who led the league in scoring for three consecutive seasons is, outside of Steph Curry, the most dominant shooter in the league. But Harden's critics say his numbers are padded by what is seen as a selfish style of play. It is another example of the complexity of his legacy.

Still, with Harden's ridiculous talent—especially offensively—it would be foolish to count him out. With the right supporting cast of teammates, Harden could easily bring multiple titles to Houston in the years to come.

# DIANA TAURASI

## WNBA **SHOOTING GUARD**  3

| | |
|---|---|
| **BIRTH YEAR** | 1982 |
| **BIRTHPLACE** | GLENDALE, CALIFORNIA |
| **HEIGHT | WEIGHT** | 6'0" | 163 LBS |
| **YEARS ACTIVE** | 2013–PRESENT |
| **TEAMS** | PHOENIX MERCURY, DYNAMO MOSCOW, SPARTAK MOSCOW ISTANBUL FENERBAHÇE S.K. GALATASARAY MEDICAL PARK UMMC EKATERINBURG |

Rookie of the Year, 2004

WNBA All-Star, 2005–2007, 2009, 2011, 2013–14, 2017–18

Finals MVP, 2009, 2014

League MVP, 2009

All-WNBA First Team, 2004, 2006–11, 2013, 2014, 2018

Scoring champion, 2006, 2008, 2009, 2010, 2011

WNBA Top 15 Players of All Time, 2011

 @BrittneyGriner

 @BrittneyYevetteGriner

## CAREER STATISTICS

(THROUGH THE 2019 SEASON)

**437**
GAMES PLAYED

**1,867**
ASSISTS

**8,575**
POINTS

**294**
BLOCKS

**1,724**
REBOUNDS

# THE BEST LONG-RANGE SHOOTER

The Phoenix Mercury were in an early 8–0 hole on the road against the Chicago Sky. They needed a spark, and Diana Taurasi gave it to them. As they brought the ball up the court, the home crowd for the Sky may not have known that a record was going to fall that night, but Mercury fans were keenly aware. What happened next embedded Taurasi deeper into conversations as the greatest to ever play the game.

As the Mercury moved the ball around looking for a clean shot against the aggressive Sky defense, Taurasi quietly slid out to three-point range. That's where team-mate Danielle Robinson found her and delivered a crisp pass. Taurasi didn't hesitate; she never even put the ball on the floor. She turned and released the quick shot before the Sky defender even had a chance to get into position. She buried the three-pointer and the record was broken—Diana Taurasi was now the all-time leading three-point shooter in WNBA history!

Though it was the 907th three-point shot of her WNBA career, Taurasi wasn't finished. When the shot dropped, it was just another bucket for the WNBA champion. She took a quick high-five from a teammate before jogging back on defense with no fanfare. She didn't come to Chicago to set personal records; she came to win the game.

Her record-setting three-pointer put Taurasi in a groove. She delivered her most dominating offensive per-formance in seven seasons, dropping 37 points on the Sky. That included matching her career high with eight three-pointers, shooting nine of 15 from the field. The record was satisfying, but for Taurasi, it was all about getting the win. She led her team back from the early deficit and returned to Phoenix with a 99–91 win.

With the victory secured, Taurasi allowed herself to reflect on her accomplishment. "Passing Katie Smith [for career three-pointers made] is something I never thought would happen," Taurasi said in an interview following the big win. "She was one of my heroes growing up. I got a chance to share the court with her at the Olympics, and she taught me how to be a professional."

The following season, Taurasi became the first player in WNBA history to reach 1,000 career three-pointers. She has continued to add to that total, proving to be the most efficient, effective long-range shooter the WNBA has ever seen.

# BECOMING THE WNBA ALL-TIME LEADING SCORER

How do you single out one moment in a career filled with 19 championships and countless record-setting performances? Is Taurasi's biggest moment her first WNBA title in 2007, when she helped lead the Mercury over the Detroit Shock in five games? How about her first of four Olympic Gold Medals, earned as a 22-year-old member of Team USA at the 2004 Games in Greece? Perhaps it would be holding her first WNBA Finals trophy in 2009 or, five years earlier, receiving the Rookie of the Year Award? In a long and dominating career filled with highlights, deciding on the highest of the highs seems arbitrary.

But the WNBA is a league driven by scoring. Fans love offense, and Taurasi has provided a ton of it during her 16-year run, so it seems fitting to look to the offensive side of the ball to highlight her biggest moment in basketball.

It was June 2018. Taurasi's Mercury were on the road to take on the Los Angeles Sparks. Taurasi was barely a week removed from breaking the WNBA three-point record. Tonight, she was chasing after the ultimate individual mark: the chance to become the all-time leading scorer in league history. Taurasi's family and friends, along with a strong showing of Mercury fans, had traveled to LA for the historic night. There was a playoff vibe in the air. Lakers great Kobe Bryant sat courtside.

Just before halftime, with her team trailing by 19 points, Taurasi made history. For the league's leading three-point shooter, it was ironic that she set the scoring record by driving the lane and rolling a layup off the glass and in. The game was stopped to celebrate Taurasi's accomplishment. Though she looked ready to get back to work, players from both teams offered on-court congratulations and she was presented with the ball. At the end of the game, Taurasi had amassed a career-total 7,494 points, passing Tina Thompson's mark of 7,488.

The Sparks spoiled Taurasi's big night, handing the Mercury a 90–59 loss. After the game, Taurasi deflected much of the praise away from herself. "It's pretty special when you pass Tina in anything, she's been such an amazing player for the WNBA and just for basketball in general, she's such an icon," Taurasi said. "And when you start thinking about more of the people that you've shared the court with, the coaches, the teams, you know I've been pretty lucky to be around a lot great players."

# JUST A KID FROM CHINO

Had things gone just a tiny bit differently, Diana Taurasi may never have scored a single WNBA point. Taurasi jokes that she could have ended up playing soccer for the United States Women's National Team. If it sounds impossible to imagine the WNBA's all-time leading scorer racing up and down a soccer pitch, consider her family history.

Taurasi's parents, Mario and Liliana, hail from the soccer-crazed country of Argentina. She and her older sister, Jessika, were raised in Chino, California, playing basketball and soccer. "The truth is, I liked soccer more," Taurasi wrote in an article for The Players' Tribune. "But my dad, knowing and encouraging, said, 'Diana. Go play basketball.'"

With a focus on soccer, Taurasi didn't even play organized basketball until she was in sixth grade. It didn't take long for people to realize she was something special on the hardwood. "In eighth grade, I got my first letter of recruitment . . . from Walla Walla Washington Community College. I was like, 'That's it! This is amazing. That's where I'm going,'" she wrote. "But more came almost every single day. I'd go to the mailbox, and there would be letters from 10, 12 schools. Places I didn't even know. Where's Drexel?

Where's Hofstra? I had no clue. I was just a kid from Chino. I didn't have any idea that the world of women's college basketball was so dense, or vast."

After a stellar high school career, during which she was named the Naismith Player of the Year in 2000, Taurasi had to choose. One thing was certain: She was going to attend a Division 1 college on a full basketball scholarship. The only question was . . . where?

Her dad wanted her to play at UConn; her mom preferred she stay closer to home. Taurasi followed dad's advice and traded California for Connecticut to become a Husky. It turned out to be the best decision of her career and maybe her life. Connecticut is a basketball powerhouse. They had just won the national championship and were known for their strong recruiting. Taurasi was the next and biggest piece in the recruiting puzzle. She would lead UConn to the Final Four in all four of her seasons as a Husky, winning three consecutive National titles. She was named Most Outstanding Player of the tournament in 2003 and 2004. Not bad for, as she liked to describe herself, "just a kid from Chino."

In 2004, UConn basketball was the talk of the sports world and Taurasi was the crown jewel of the program. That's why it came as no surprise when the Phoenix Mercury used the number one pick in the 2004 WNBA Draft to bring Taurasi to Arizona.

# AN UNDISPUTED LEADER ON THE COURT

Professional sports offer a short career. Players who do stick around often do so by jumping from team to team, filling the needs of different organizations. The Mercury coaches and executives could never have imagined when they signed Taurasi that 16 years later she would still be with the organization and performing at an elite level. It was, in hindsight, the best draft pick in league history. And Taurasi didn't waste any time proving the Mercury made the right choice. In her WNBA debut against the Sacramento Monarchs, Taurasi was, in the words of Monarchs head coach John Whisenant, "awesome."

Fittingly, the first shot she took—and made—in her career was a three-pointer. She showed her versatility with several nifty assists, three blocks, and a highlight reel half-court shot that she drained at the buzzer before the half. The Mercury fell short in the game, but it was clear to the more than 10,000 fans that packed the arena that something special had come to Phoenix.

From her rookie season forward, Taurasi established herself as the undisputed leader of the Mercury. Her head coach, Sandy Brondello, speaks regularly about what it means to have Taurasi on the squad. "Diana Taurasi is just amazing," Brondello says. "She's a great leader and, she'll lead through action or she'll lead though constructive criticism or motivation. Whatever it takes, that's what she'll do. She'll drive people to get better."

Look at Game 3 of the 2014 WNBA Finals. Taurasi's Mercury led Elena Delle Donne's Chicago Sky 3–2 in the best of five series. But the Sky were at home for Game 3, hoping to keep the series alive. The two teams battled it out for 39 minutes, and with the game tied at 82–82 and less than 20 seconds left on the clock, both teams needed a clutch play. Taurasi delivered.

Bringing the ball up the court, any other player might have been tempted to stay on the perimeter, milk the clock, and look for a long-range shot for the game-winner. Instead, Taurasi drove to the basket for the tough pull-up jumper. In a hostile environment, with an aggressive defender on her and the game on the line, Taurasi delivered the game-winner! Adding icing to the cake, she drew the foul and converted the three-point play, giving the Mercury the 85–82 lead. With the Mercury star center Brittney Griner out with an injury, Taurasi put the team on her back and delivered her third title to Phoenix.

# A SUCCESSFUL CAREER THAT SPANS THE GLOBE

To play professional basketball for a single game means you are an elite athlete and one of the best players in the world. To play at the highest level for 16 years (and counting) like Taurasi has is a tribute to her physical gifts, her mental toughness, and her passion for the game. That collectively shapes a large part of her legacy. When examining her legacy, there is value in simple longevity.

Taurasi will also be remembered as a proven winner. She stands in rare air, having won championships in four different professional leagues. In addition to leading the Mercury to the WNBA Championship title three times, she was part of seven title-winning teams in the Russian National League, she collected six trophies in the EuroLeague, and she won a title in the Turkish National League in 2011. Add in her three National Championships at UConn and Taurasi is one of the most decorated basketball players in history.

Like so many of her peers in women's basketball, Taurasi is also known for her advocacy work. She has long been outspoken for LGBTQ rights, and more recently she has joined the fight to gain a more equitable sharing of league revenue with the players. In 2019, Taurasi earned the league maximum salary of $117,500 playing for the Mercury. She earned $1.5 million playing in the Russian National League. Taurasi has been one of the most vocal players in the WNBA when it comes to criticizing the pay scale. "We had to go to a communist country to get paid like capitalists," she said in a 2019 interview. "Which is so backward to everything that was in the history books in sixth grade."

Taurasi was the first WNBA star to sit out a full WNBA season because of salary. In 2015, her Russian squad, UMMC Ekaterinburg, requested that she sit out the season to rest her body. Considering the Russian team paid her roughly 14 times more than the WNBA, it seemed like a reasonable request. Taurasi sat, and that will forever be etched in her legacy. She was called selfish by fans, who accused her of quitting on her teammates. But within the league, she received support from other players for her decision to protect herself and her career first.

Nevertheless, Taurasi is known for her unending drive. She has battled back from hip, back, and ankle injuries, always pushing herself harder in rehab to rejoin her teammates. The injuries are thought to be caused, in part, by the year-round schedule she keeps. In addition to playing extended seasons in the WNBA when Phoenix makes the playoffs, Taurasi has built a second superstar career overseas. The pay is great (especially compared to WNBA salaries), but the wear and tear on her body adds up.

When she steps away from the game, Diana Taurasi will be remembered as one of the best—if not *the* best—to play the game. She will be remembered for her deadly three-point shooting ability, her passion for the game of basketball, and her ability to win wherever she goes. She will be remembered by many as simply the G.O.A.T.

# HONORABLE MENTIONS
## SHOOTING GUARDS

## DONOVAN MITCHELL

As the youngest player in this book, Mitchell earns a spot among the game's greats by virtue of the red-hot start to his NBA career. As a rookie, Mitchell started 71 games for the Utah Jazz in 2017–18, posting more than 20 points per game. Historically, rookies can wear down by the end of the long NBA season and then struggle in the playoffs. For

Mitchell, it was just the opposite. In the 2017–18 playoffs, he lit it up, putting up 171 points in the first playoff series of his career. Only Kareem Abdul-Jabbar and Wilt Chamberlain posted better scoring numbers to begin their playoff careers.

Jazz coach Quin Snyder offered high praise for Mitchell's play in the midst of his first trip to the playoffs. "I [didn't] see Donovan as a rookie for the most part, for the whole season," Snyder said, "because of the way he's played and the poise he's had . . . the way he's elevated his teammates."

Mitchell's strong start wasn't a one-hit wonder. He came back in the 2019 playoffs, scoring 21 points per game. Through his first two seasons, Mitchell averaged 23.4 points per game in the postseason. At 23 years old, Mitchell looks to be one of the exciting young players to watch in the NBA for years to come.

# JRUE HOLIDAY

While many of the players in this book are noted for their offensive abilities, New Orleans Pelicans star Jrue Holiday is coveted for his defensive skills. The 11-year NBA veteran is a shutdown defender, often drawing the opponent's best player. Holiday doesn't post flashy offensive numbers (averaging 15 points per game over his career), and he played much of the time in the shadow of superstar Anthony Davis before Davis was traded to the Lakers in 2019. Still, when Holiday is on the floor, his team is better.

Holiday had his best season as a pro in 2018–19. With Davis missing 26 games as he forced his way out of New Orleans, Holiday elevated his game. He posted career highs in points per game (21.7) and rebounds per game (five). Holiday's 2018–19 season was filled with plenty of highlights, but an early season game at home against the Brooklyn Nets personified his clutch play.

The Pelicans were trailing 115–114 with seven seconds to go as Holiday took the inbounds pass. He didn't panic. Instead, he worked his way to the top of the key. He began to drive the lane, then pulled up at the foul line and took the fadeaway jumper. He buried the shot, and the Nets won, 116–115!

## JEWELL LOYD

The Seattle Storm invested the first overall draft pick on Jewell Loyd in 2015, and Loyd hasn't disappointed. The year before she arrived in Seattle, the Storm had a record of 12–22 and missed the playoffs. Just four seasons later, Loyd led the Storm to the WNBA Championship.

The former Notre Dame standout has been a dependable player for the Storm, playing in every game of her first four years in the league. The five-foot-ten guard has averaged nearly 15 points per game in her career. She is also money from the free throw line. In a 2015 game against the Washington Mystics, Loyd set a franchise record by hitting 14–14 from the line. Her perfection helped the Storm come back from a 14-point deficit to win the game.

Free throws are nice, but legacies are made in the playoffs. In the 2018 Finals, Loyd came out on fire. She led all scorers in Game 1 with 23 points. Thanks to her dominance, the Storm won the game and never looked back. They swept the Mystics 3–0 to take the title.

# LEGENDARY GREAT
## SHOOTING GUARD

## MICHAEL JORDAN

The idea of reducing the value of Michael Jordan to the game of basketball down to a few hundred words is comically impossible. Dozens of books and documentaries have chronicled every aspect of Jordan's life on and off the basketball court. If he isn't the greatest basketball player that ever lived, then he is standing just a half-step behind LeBron James on the mountaintop.

Many fans already have an appreciation for the man they call simply "M. J." Rather than trying to single out a game or two from the endless clutch moments, buzzer beaters, and monster performances of his career to demonstrate his value, let's instead get a sense of the impact he had not only on the game of basketball, but also on the world around him.

His legend transcends generations. His high-flying dunks, with tongue sticking out, were often imitated and rarely replicated. He had millions of kids on playgrounds around the world trying to "be like Mike." Every time he touched the basketball, fans expected something special to happen. There was seemingly no shot he couldn't make. Half-court buzzer beaters were a regular occurrence. He shot over double-teams with ease. He was equally comfortable driving into the paint and banging bodies as he was gracefully arcing a long-distance three-pointer.

In a game that is incredibly fast, Jordan made it seem leisurely, almost easy at times. He often looked like he had another gear the other players on the court were missing, as though he could see three moves ahead and anticipate what his opponent was going to do next. He was, for many years, unstoppable.

Jordan was such an athletic talent that he took a season off mid-career and played professional baseball. (He signed a minor-league contract with the Chicago White Sox in 1994.) Jordan knocked in 51 runs, stole 30 bases, and sold out every stadium he played in. Then, as though he never left, he returned to the Chicago Bulls and led them to three titles over the next four seasons.

But legendary players are measured beyond the court as well. Jordan has donated tens of millions of dollars to various charities in his lifetime. He has supported children's programs and worked to provide opportunities for those living in the inner city. He built and funded a Boys & Girls Club in Chicago, which he named after his late father.

One of Jordan's most enduring gestures came in 2001. After the September 11 terrorist attacks, Jordan announced he was donating his entire salary for the 2001–02 season to support the families who lost loved ones in the attacks. At the time, Jordan said simply, "It's my way of giving back and hopefully aiding those in need during a terrible time."

Although this segment opened by outlining why M. J.'s value as a legend couldn't be summed up in a few stats and game highlights, here is a taste of "Air Jordan" by the numbers: 32,292 points; 6,672 rebounds; 5,633 assists; six NBA Championship titles; five league MVP awards; and six Finals MVP awards.

Jordan led the league in scoring 10 times and holds the record for the most playoff games scoring 40 or more points. He did it an incredible 38 times! Today he is known as the owner of the Charlotte Bobcats and the namesake of Air Jordan shoes, but for a generation of basketball fans, he was simply the greatest.

# Create Your Own
# Fantasy Team

**C**

**SF**

**PF**

**PG**

**SG**

# WNBA TEAM

**C**

**SF**

**PF**

**PG**

**SG**

# RESOURCES & REFERENCES

Note: All statistics used in the intro boxes for each player, as well as awards, all-star appearances, etc., were collected from basketball-reference.com unless otherwise noted. All NBA statistics were through the end of the 2018–19 season only.

## 1. NBA CENTER: *JOEL EMBIID*

Behrens, Tanner. "Joel Embiid." Beyond the Single Story (blog), March 27, 2018. https://beyondthesinglestory.wordpress.com/2018/03/27/joel-embiid.

Decourcy, Mike. "Joel Embiid's Pursuit of Hoops Greatness Not Just a Dream." Sporting News, January 22, 2014. https://www.sportingnews.com/us/ncaa-basketball/news/joel-embiids-pursuit-of-hoops-greatness-not-just-a-dream/wxyk1v6zv97t1pep47qnkyv1y.

ESPN. "Joel Embiid." https://www.espn.com/nba/player/_/id/3059318/joel-embiid.

FreeDawkins. "Joel Embiid Full Highlights 2016.12.18 vs Nets - 33 Pts, 10 Rebs, 3 Blks, 2 GOOD!" YouTube, December 18, 2016. https://www.youtube.com/watch?v=Dcqkwd0BL9k.

FreeDawkins. "MASKED Joel Embiid Playoffs DEBUT 2018 ECR1 Game 3 Philadelphia 76ers vs Miami Heat - 23 Pts, 7 Rebs, 4 Asts, 3 Blks!" YouTube, April 19, 2018. https://www.youtube.com/watch?v=-0FwMcqjVIU.

House of Highlights. "Joel Embiid Postgame Press Conference | Sixers vs Heat - Game 3 | April 19, 2018 | 2018 NBA Playoffs." YouTube, April 19, 2018. https://www.youtube.com/watch?v=QbQgkn9Tg2w.

Kansas Athletics. "Joel Embiid." https://kuathletics.com/roster/joel-embiid.

Skipper, Clay. "Joel Embiid Is Seven Feet Tall and Rising." *GQ*, October 22, 2018. https://www.gq.com/story/joel-embiid-digital-cover.

VICE Sports. "Joel Embiid's Rise to NBA Stardom." *The Way We Ball - In Partnership with the NBA* S1: E1. September 25, 2018. https://www.youtube.com/watch?v=vlwtwUnwzqg.

## 2. WNBA CENTER: *BRITTNEY GRINER*

Baylor University. "Brittney Griner." https://baylorbears.com/sports/womens-basketball/roster/brittney-griner/3266.

ESPN. "Brittney Griner discusses being gay." April 18, 2013. https://www.espn.com/wnba/story/_/id/9185633/brittney-griner-comes-says-just-are.

*HuffPost*. "Brittney Griner, Openly Gay WNBA Star, Opens Up About Bullying And Being A Role Model." Last modified February 2, 2016. https://www.huffpost.com/entry/brittney-griner-bullying_n_3617907?guccounter=1.

Jordan, Jason. "Brittney Griner's HS coach says she'll go down as the greatest of all time." High School Sports (*USA Today*), March 19, 2015. https://usatodayhss.com/2015/brittney-griner-phoenix-mercury-griner-brittney-griner-dunk-nimitz-brittney-griner-wnba.

Olympic. "USA win women's Basketball gold again." YouTube, August 24, 2016. https://www.youtube.com/watch?v=YyhhpFSPKMc.

Rohlin, Melissa. "WNBA's Brittney Griner has learned to rise above it all." *Los Angeles Times*, July 17, 2013. https://www.latimes.com/sports/la-xp m-2013-jul-17-la-sp-brittney-griner-20130718-story.html.

Tapper, Christina M. "Baylor Superstar Brittney Griner Talks About When She Was a Kid." *Sports Illustrated Kids*, March 22, 2013. https:// www.sikids.com/from-the-mag/brittney-griner-being-kid.

Wolfman-Arent, Avi. "2012 Olympics: Brittney Griner Says No to Team USA." Bleacher Report, April 19, 2012. https://bleacherreport.com/arti cles/1152579-brittney-griner-says-no-to-team-usa-wont-play-in-2012-lo ndon-olympics.

WNBA. "Brittney Griner Debuts for the Phoenix Mercury!" YouTube, May 27, 2013. https://www.youtube.com/watch?v=3kuM5kJdqGg.

WNBA. "Brittney Griner speaks after winning her 1st Championship!" YouTube, September 12, 2014. https://www.youtube.com/ watch?v=OoimfVv78.

# HONORABLE MENTIONS

## *ANTHONY DAVIS*

ESPN. "Anthony Davis." https://www.espn.com/nba/player/_/id/6583/ anthony-davis.

Wells, Adam. "Report: Anthony Davis Traded to Lakers for Lonzo Ball, Brandon Ingram, More." Bleacher Report, June 15, 2019. https:// bleacherreport.com/articles/2755098-report-anthony-davis-traded-to-lake rs-for-lonzo-ball-brandon-ingram-more.

## *NIKOLA JOKIĆ*

Goldberg, Rob. "Nikola Jokic, Nuggets Reportedly to Agree to 5-Year, $148M Contract Extension." Bleacher Report, June 30, 2018. https://bleacherreport.com/articles/2782863-nikola-jokic-nuggets-reportedly-to-agree-to-5-year-148m-contract-extension.

## *LEGENDARY GREAT: KAREEM ABDUL-JABBAR*

Van Dusen, Ryan. "Kareem Abdul-Jabbar - 1989 NBA Finals Highlights (42 Years Old)." YouTube, 4:17, August 10, 2016. https://www.youtube.com/watch?v=JwTyxXPr8gY&t=256s.

# 3. NBA SMALL FORWARD: *KAWHI LEONARD*

Abrams, Jonathan. "The Making of Kawhi Leonard, the Silent Superstar." Bleacher Report, April 4, 2017. https://bleacherreport.com/articles/2700300-the-making-of-kawhi-leonard-the-silent-superstar.

Ford, Chad. "Pacers acquire guard George Hill." ESPN, June 23, 2011. https://www.espn.com/nba/draft2011/news/story?id=6698432.

NBA. "76ERS vs RAPTORS | JAW-DROPPING End to Series Finale! | Game 7." YouTube, May 12, 2019. https://www.youtube.com/watch?v=7CyFymdSZ2E.

Rapp, Timothy. "Kawhi Leonard Reportedly Could Sit Out, Has 'No Interest' in Raptors After Trade." Bleacher Report, July 18, 2018. https://bleacherreport.com/articles/2786698-kawhi-leonard-reportedly-could-sit-out-has-no-interest-in-raptors-after-trade.

San Diego State University. "Kawhi Leonard." https://goaztecs.com/sports/mens-basketball/roster/kawhi-leonard/565.

Schwartz, Nick. "What's going on with Kawhi Leonard: A strange timeline." For the Win (*USA Today*), July 18, 2018. https://ftw.usatoday.com/2018/07/whats-going-on-with-kawhi-leonard-a-strange-timeline.

Sondheimer, Eric. "Shooting Death of His Father Drives Riverside King's Leonard." *Los Angeles Times*, September 16, 2014. https://www.latimes.com/sports/la-sp-sondheimer8mar08-column.html.

Uggetti, Paolo. "The Real L.A. Stories of Kawhi Leonard and Paul George." The Ringer, October 3, 2019. https://www.theringer.com/nba-preview/2019/10/3/20895966/kawhi-leonard-paul-george-los-angeles-clippers-stories-growing-up.

## 4. WNBA SMALL FORWARD: *ELENA DELLE DONNE*

Brodesser-Akner, Taffy. "The Audacity of Height." ESPN, November 22, 2016. http://www.espn.com/espn/feature/story/_/page/espnw-delledonne161122/chicago-sky-elena-delle-donne-spent-years-learning-accept-height.

Byrum, Tyler. "Elena Delle Donne wins her first championship despite three herniated discs in her back." NBC Sports, October 10, 2019. https://www.nbcsports.com/washington/wizards/elena-delle-donne-wins-her-first-championship-despite-three-herniated-discs-her-back.

Chase. "Elena Delle Donne on Finances, Family, Health and Equal Pay | Kneading Dough S.2 E.5." YouTube, October 19, 2018. https://www.youtube.com/watch?v=Xdef_HjeyPE.

Elena Delle Donne. https://elenadelledonne.com.

ESPN. "Elena Delle Donne returning to U.S. after Lyme disease flare-up." Associated Press. https://www.espn.com/wnba/story/_/id/18552312/elena-delle-donne-heading-back-us-china-lyme-disease-flare-up?device=featurephone.

Ginsburg, David. "Delaware star Delle Donne has no regrets about leaving UConn." *Star Tribune*, March 21, 2013. http://www.startribune.com/delaware-star-delle-donne-has-no-regrets-about-leaving-uconn/199457221.

Maloney, Jack. "WNBA Finals 2019: Elena Delle Donne's back injury has massive impact on Mystics' Game 2 loss to Sun." CBS Sports, October 1, 2019. https://www.cbssports.com/wnba/news/wnba-finals-2019-elena-delle-donnes-back-injury-has-massive-impact-on-mystics-game-2-loss-to-sun.

Schroeder, Jessa. "'I love a woman, it is no big deal': WNBA star Elena Delle Donne marries girlfriend Amanda Clifton in lavish ceremony." *Daily Mail*, November 4, 2017. https://www.dailymail.co.uk/news/article-5049019/WNBA-star-Elena-Delle-Donne-marries-Amanda-Clifton.html.

Smith, Bryan. "The New Superstar in Town." *Chicago*, May 16, 2016. https://www.chicagomag.com/Chicago-Magazine/June-2016/Elena-Delle-Donne.

Spruill, Tamryn. "Hoops Happening: Elena Delle Donne, 'Uninterrupted': 'Women aren't valued the same way that men are in the workforce.'" Swish Appeal (SB Nation), October 16, 2018. https://www.swishappeal.com/2018/10/16/17976324/elena-delle-donne-nba-wnba-pay-equity-uninterrupted-maverick-carter.

Voepel, Mechelle. "Family comes first for Delle Donne, even during WNBA championship run." ESPN, October 7, 2019. https://www.espn.com/wnba/story/_/id/27792827/family-comes-first-delle-donne-even-wnba-championship-run.

WNBA. "Griner and Delle Donne Go Head-to-Head in Their WNBA Debuts!" YouTube, May 27, 2013. https://www.youtube.com/watch?v=-6twUg70OEM.

# HONORABLE MENTIONS

### JIMMY BUTLER

NBA. "Reports: Minnesota Timberwolves trade Jimmy Butler to 76ers." November 10, 2018. https://www.nba.com/article/2018/10/04/report-minnesota-timberwolves-trade-butler-76ers.

Rapp, Timothy. "Jimmy Butler Talks 76ers Tenure, Says Some Teammates Didn't Work as Hard as Him." Bleacher Report, November 27, 2019. https://bleacherreport.com/articles/2864509-jimmy-butler-talks-76ers-tenure-says-some-teammates-didnt-work-as-hard-as-him.

### KLAY THOMPSON

Goldberg, Rob. "Warriors Rumors: Klay Thompson Ready to Agree on 5-Year, $190M Contract with GS." Bleacher Report, June 26, 2019. https://bleacherreport.com/articles/2842944-warriors-rumors-klay-thompson-ready-to-agree-on-5-year-190m-contract-with-gs.

Shapiro, Michel. "Watch: Klay Thompson Sets NBA Record with 14 Threes vs. Bulls." *Sports Illustrated*, October 29, 2018. https://www.si.com/nba/2018/10/30/klay-thompson-nba-record-14-threes.

## MAYA MOORE

Nelson, Ryne. "Maya Moore Talks Motivation, Offseason and Dominant Minnesota Lynx Run." *SLAM*, September 26, 2018. https://www.slamonline.com/wnba/maya-moore-appreciative-dominant-minnesota-lynx-run.

## LEGENDARY GREAT: LARRY BIRD

Gelso, Nick. "Larry Bird: The Sudden and Saddening Demise Of a Basketball Legend." Bleacher Report, July 31, 2009. https://bleacherreport.com/articles/228427-larry-bird-the-sudden-and-saddening-demise-of-a-basketball-legend.

# 5. NBA POWER FORWARD: *LEBRON JAMES*

Gaines, Cork. "LEBRON JAMES: How the king of the NBA spends his millions." Business Insider, May 10, 2019. https://www.businessinsider.com/how-lebron-spends-his-money-2016-6.

Hector, Jarod. "High School Jersey Worn By LeBron James For 'Sports Illustrated' Cover Shoot Up For Auction." BET, September 30, 2019. https://www.bet.com/news/sports/2019/09/30/high-school-jersey-worn-by-lebron-james-for-sports-illustrated-c.html.

Helfand, Zach. "LeBron James Never Forgot Where He Came from, and They Never Forgot Him." *Los Angeles Times*, October 27, 2014. https://www.latimes.com/sports/nba/la-sp-lebron-james-akron-20141028-story.html.

House of Highlights. "The Game MASKED LeBron James BECAME a LEGEND 2014.03.03 vs Bobcats - 61 Points, EPIC NIGHT!" YouTube, August 12, 2018. https://www.youtube.com/watch?v=O5PRGB1Khts.

House of Highlights. "LeBron James Back-To-Back Championship, Game 7 Highlights vs Spurs 2013 Finals - 37 Pts, CLUTCH HD." YouTube, June 14, 2018. https://www.youtube.com/watch?v=hDDzmksK4fw.

House of Highlights. "LeBron James First NBA Game, Full Highlights vs Kings (2003.10.29) - MUST WATCH Debut! HD." YouTube, June 19, 2018. https://www.youtube.com/watch?v=JLjH0rrNFeU.

NBA. "LeBron James becomes first player in NBA history with triple-doubles vs. 30 teams." November 20, 2019. https://www.nba.com/article/2019/11/20/lebron-james-becomes-firs t-post-triple-double-vs-30-teams.

Saslow, Eli. "Lost stories of LeBron, part 1." ESPN, October 17, 2013. https://www.espn.com/nba/story/_/id/9825052/how-lebron-james-lif e-changed-fourth-grade-espn-magazine.

Shontell, Alyson, and Arielle Berger. "LeBron James created a foundation that has pledged to give more than 1,100 students full rides to college, which could cost ~ $41 million." Business Insider, August 22, 2016. https://www.businessinsider.com/lebron-james-family-foundation-interview -kids-education-college-2016-8.

## 6. WNBA POWER FORWARD: *CANDACE PARKER*

Johnson, Martenzie. "'Get Back into the Kitchen': A WNBA Roundtable on Sexism in Basketball." The Undefeated, August 20, 2018. https://theundefeated.com/features/wnba-roundtable-on-sexism-in-basketbal l-imani-mcgee-stafford-devereaux-peters-mistie-bass-elena-delle-donne-aj a-wilson-candace-parker.

Jordan, Jason. "Girls Sports Month: A look back at Candace Parker in high school." High School Sports (*USA Today*), March 14, 2018. https://usatodayhss.com/2018/girls-sports-month-a-look-back-at-candace-parker-in-high-school.

NBA. "Candace Parker Has the Best Rookie Debut in WNBA History." YouTube, May 18, 2008. https://www.youtube.com/watch?v=HsCks-kBfKc.

Nesfeder, Mary Paige. "WNBA Star Candace Parker Doesn't Want To Be One Of The Boys." Refinery29, June 21, 2019. https://www.refinery29.com/en-us/candace-parker-wnba-gender-equality-basketball-interview.

USA Basketball. "Before They Made It: Candace Parker." March 21, 2014. https://www.usab.com/news-events/news/2014/03/before-they-made-it-candace-parker.aspx.

WNBA. "American Express Off the Court 2014 WNBA All-Star Roundtable." YouTube, July 19, 2014. https://www.youtube.com/watch?v=7GvWkODKkVE.

WNBA. "Lisa Leslie and Candace Parker Reflect On Their In Game Dunks." YouTube, March 13, 2017. https://www.youtube.com/watch?v=TnlmU68Lku0.

Women's Basketball Daily. "WNBA Final Game 5 Los Angeles Sparks Minnesota Lynx 20 10 16." YouTube, December 18, 2016. https://www.youtube.com/watch?v=zmS3fds64ms.

# HONORABLE MENTIONS

### GIANNIS ANTETOKOUNMPO

Goodman, Peter S. "Giannis Antetokounmpo Is the Pride of a Greece That Shunned Him." *New York Times*, May 3, 2019. https://www.nytimes.com/2019/05/03/sports/giannis-antetokounmpo-greece.html.

### BLAKE GRIFFIN

Daniels, Tim. "Blake Griffin Traded to Pistons for Avery Bradley, Tobias Harris and More." Bleacher Report, January 29, 2018. https://bleacherreport.com/articles/2614395-report-blake-griffin-traded-to-pistons-for-avery-bradley-tobias-harris-more.

Love, Ryan. "Pistons doomsday scenario: What if Blake Griffin can't come back?" FanSided, November 1, 2019. https://pistonpowered.com/2019/11/01/pistons-doomsday-scenario-what-if-blake-griffin-cant-come-back.

NBA. "Blake Griffin Sets a NEW Career High 50 Points vs Sixers | October 23, 2018." YouTube, October 23, 2018. https://www.youtube.com/watch?v=vxYBsUdosGo.

### LEGENDARY GREAT: TIM DUNCAN

NBA. "Tim Duncan's San Antonio Spurs Jersey Retirement (Full Ceremony)." YouTube, December 19, 2016. https://www.youtube.com/watch?v=WaZSfGTeqhQ&t=1436s.

## 7. NBA POINT GUARD: *STEPHEN CURRY*

Becker, Jon. "Remember when Stephen Curry's ankle injuries threatened his career?" *The Mercury News*, last modified December 6, 2017. https://www.mercurynews.com/2017/12/05/remember-when-stephen-curry s-ankle-injuries-threatened-his-career.

Davis, Scott. "Stephen Curry shared an anecdote that shows how unlikely his NBA ascent has been." Business Insider, June 9, 2017. https://www.businessinsider.com/stephen-curry-high-schoo l-unlikely-nba-career-2017-6.

Golden State Warriors. "Warriors Introduce Stephen Curry." YouTube, June 29, 2009. https://www.youtube.com/watch?v=qZwUn6mF9Ic.

NBA. "Steph and Dell Curry Share Special NBA Bond on Father's Day." YouTube, June 20, 2015. https://www.youtube.com/ watch?v=PEphPunTjRM.

NBA. "Steph Curry Drains the Game Winner vs Oklahoma City." YouTube, February 27, 2016. https://www.youtube.com/ watch?v=GEMVGHoenXM.

NBA. "Stephen Curry Named Unanimous Winner of 2015-16 Kia NBA Most Valuable Player Award." May 10, 2016. https://www.nba.com/ warriors/news/curry-mvp-20160510.

TODAY. "Stephen Curry Responds to Being Called 'The Greatest Basketball Player of All Time': Full Interview." YouTube, 19:46, April 3, 2019. https://www.youtube.com/watch?v=6S25PgJshPc&t=1186s.

## 8. WNBA POINT GUARD: *SUE BIRD*

Associated Press. "Bird becomes first guard to go No. 1." ESPN, April 19, 2002. http://www.espn.com/wnba/news/2002/0419/1371034.html.

Bird, Sue. "So the President F*cking Hates My Girlfriend." The Players' Tribune, July 2, 2019. https://www.theplayerstribune.com/en-us/articles/sue-bird-megan-rapinoe-uswnt.

Classic Basketball. "2001 Big East Championship Notre Dame vs Connecticut." YouTube, January 7, 2015. https://www.youtube.com/watch?v=swZsMh3qs60.

Griffus, Annette. "NEW YORK 78, SEATTLE 61: Storm learn from, and lose to, Liberty." *Kitsap Sun*, May 31, 2002. https://products.kitsapsun.com/archive/2002/05-31/0060_new_york_78__seattle_61__storm_le.html.

JockBio.com. "Sue Bird." http://www.jockbio.com/Bios/Bird/Bird_bio.html.

Ramachandran, Preetha. "WNBA star Sue Bird discusses sports equality at event." *The Chronicle*, September 17, 2019. https://www.dukechronicle.com/article/2019/09/wnba-sue-bird-sports-equality-duke-university.

Seymour, Emma. "The Danger of Low Pay in the WNBA." *Ms.*, April 23, 2019. https://msmagazine.com/2019/04/23/the-danger-of-low-pay-i n-the-wnba.

UConn Hoop Legends. "Sue Bird." http://www.uconnhooplegends.com/womensledgends/BirdSue.html.

WNBA. "Game 1 - 2010 WNBA Finals - Dream 77, Storm 79 (F)." YouTube, September 14, 2010. https://www.youtube.com/watch?v=He6T2nnPQbs.

WNBA. "Hoops 101: Sue Bird." https://www.wnba.com/archive/wnba/chats_mailboxes/hoops101_bird.html.

WNBA. "Sue Bird To Miss Remainder of 2019 WNBA Season." September 3, 2019. https://storm.wnba.com/news/sue-bird-to-miss-remainder-of-2019-wnba-season.

# HONORABLE MENTIONS

### RUSSELL WESTBROOK

Ellentuck, Matt. "There's only 1 winner in the blockbuster Russell Westbrook trade to the Rockets." SB Nation, July 12, 2019. https://www.sbnation.com/2019/7/12/20691259/russell-westbrook-trade-rockets-chris-paul-winners-losers.

NBA. "Westbrook averages triple-double for third straight season." April 5, 2019. https://www.nba.com/article/2019/04/05/westbrook-averages-triple-double-third-straight-season.

### KYRIE IRVING

House of Highlights. "Kyrie Irving AMAZING Brooklyn Nets Debut Full Highlights vs Timberwolves (2019.10.23) - 50 Points!" YouTube, October 23, 2019. https://www.youtube.com/watch?v=B1r6tgpxEwk.

### *COURTNEY VANDERSLOOT*

Basketball Reference. "WNBA Year-by-Year Leaders and Records for Assists Per Game." https://www.basketball-reference.com/wnba/leaders/ast_per_g_yearly.html.

Kenney, Madeline. "Sky point guard Courtney Vandersloot earns third consecutive peak performer award." *Chicago Sun Times*, September 9, 2019. https://chicago.suntimes.com/chicago-sky-and-wnba/2019/9/9/20857600/sky-pg-courtney-vandersloot-earns-third-consecutive-peak-performer-award.

### *LEGENDARY GREAT: **MAGIC JOHNSON***

House of Highlights. "Rookie Magic Johnson Full Game 6 Highlights vs 76ers (1980 NBA Finals) - 42 Pts, 15 Reb, FINALS MVP!" YouTube, August 14, 2018. https://www.youtube.com/watch?v=H906s1BZu-Y.

## **9.** NBA SHOOTING GUARD: *JAMES HARDEN*

Associated Press. "James Harden gets $80 million." ESPN, October 31, 2012. https://www.espn.com/nba/story/_/id/8577246/james-harden-houston-rockets-agree-five-year-80-million-contract.

ESPN. "James Harden 'happy' he gave Madison Square Garden career-high 61 points in Rockets' win | NBA Sound." YouTube, January 23, 2019. https://www.youtube.com/watch?v=Q4260CIx6uw.

EYESOLD NBA. "James Harden Shocks Entire World with CRAZIEST Game Winner! Warriors vs Rockets Insane Final Minutes." YouTube, January 3, 2019. https://www.youtube.com/watch?v=bVzQJoiWXIk.

Hughes, Grant. "Criticism Reaching Critical Mass for James Harden, But Is It Fair?" Bleacher Report, February 23, 2016. https://bleacherreport.com/articles/2619012-criticism-reaching-critical-mass-for-james-harden-but-is-it-fair.

NBA. "James Harden Drops a CAREER-HIGH 61 Points In New York." YouTube, January 23, 2019. https://www.youtube.com/watch?v=awsMi_28GN8.

NBA. "James Harden's UNBELIEVABLE Clutch 61 Point Performance | March 22, 2019." YouTube, March 22, 2019. https://www.youtube.com/watch?v=MyKqMDdic-o.

Spears, Marc J. "Rockets' James Harden and His Mom on How Sports Shaped the MVP Candidate." The Undefeated, May 5, 2017. https://theundefeated.com/features/rockets-james-harden-and-mom-sports-shaped-mvp-candidate.

## 10. WNBA SHOOTING GUARD: *DIANA TAURASI*

Altman, Lee. "Diana Taurasi Extends Claim Over Record Books." NBA, June 2, 2017. http://global.nba.com/news/diana-taurasi-extends-claim-over-record-books.

Heavren, Natalie. "Diana Taurasi (mostly) welcomed back by Connecticut." FanSided, July 13, 2019. https://highposthoops.com/2019/07/13/connecticut-sun-spoil-diana-taurasis-return.

Killian, Tyler. "Diana Taurasi to sit out 2015 WNBA season after accepting Russian team offer." *USA Today*, February 3, 2015. https://www.usatoday.com/story/sports/wnba/mercury/2015/02/03/diana-taurasi-to-miss-2015-season/22816013.

Negley, Cassandra. "Diana Taurasi: WNBA players have to 'go to a communist country to get paid like capitalists.'" Yahoo! Sports, July 24, 2019. https://sports.yahoo.com/diana-taurasi-wnba-players-have-to-go -to-a-communist-country-to-get-paid-like-capitalists-203718592.html.

Staff. "Phoenix Mercury earn third WNBA title, defeating Chicago Sky 87-82." Hoopfeed, September 13, 2014. https://www.hoopfeed.com/ content/2014/09/phoenix-mercury-earn-third-wnba-title-defeating-ch icago-sky-87-82.

Taurasi, Diana. "Just a Kid from Chino." The Players' Tribune, September 2, 2015. https://www.theplayerstribune.com/en-us/articles/ just-a-kid-from-chino.

Thakker, Krishna. "Diana Taurasi Breaks WNBA Scoring Record." *Fortune*, June 19, 2017. https://fortune.com/2017/06/19/diana-tauras i-wnba-scoring-record.

WNBA. "History: Diana Taurasi Becomes WNBA's All-Time Leading Scorer." YouTube, June 18, 2017. https://www.youtube.com/ watch?v=-cz3ZC6QkpM.

WNBA. "2014 WNBA Finals Game 3 Minimovie." YouTube, 2:45, September 14, 2014. https://www.youtube.com/ watch?v=f2_bmncW-UQ&t=165s.

# HONORABLE MENTIONS

## DONOVAN MITCHELL

NBA on ESPN. "[FULL] Quin Snyder says he doesn't view Donovan Mitchell as a rookie | NBA on ESPN." YouTube, April 15, 2018. https:// www.youtube.com/watch?v=RHb_3P0Mhug.

## JRUE HOLIDAY

House of Highlights. "Jrue Holiday GAME-WINNER | Nets vs Pelicans | October 26, 2018 | 2018-19 NBA Season." YouTube, October 26, 2018. https://www.youtube.com/watch?v=3K0gDRK4_RQ.

## JEWELL LOYD

Basketball Reference. "Jewell Loyd WNBA Stats." https://www.basketball-reference.com/wnba/players/l/loydje01w.html.

Basketball Reference. "2014 Seattle Storm Stats." https://www.basketball-reference.com/wnba/teams/SEA/2014.html.

Evans, Jayda. "Rookie Jewell Loyd leads the way as Storm beats Mystics, 69-59." *The Seattle Times*, August 30, 2015. https://www.seattletimes.com/sports/storm/rookie-loyd-leads-the-way-as-storm-beats-mystics-69-59.

WNBA. "Emerald City: Seattle Selects Loyd With No. 1 Overall Pick." August 16, 2015. https://www.wnba.com/draft2015.

WNBA. "WNBA Playoffs 2018." https://www.wnba.com/playoffs2018.

## LEGENDARY GREAT: MICHAEL JORDAN

Baseball Reference. "Michael Jordan." https://www.baseball-reference.com/register/player.fcgi?id=jordan001mic.

Boys & Girls Clubs of Chicago. "James R. Jordan Boys & Girls Club." https://bgcc.org/james-r-jordan-club.

CNN.com/U.S. "Jordan to donate his salary for relief efforts." October 17, 2001. http://edition.cnn.com/2001/US/10/17/rec.jordan.salary.

# ACKNOWLEDGMENTS

It takes a village to build a book, and it takes an even bigger village to build a writer who builds a book. Thanks to the many people who have helped me along the way, both in my career as a writer and specifically on this project. There are too many to name, but I'll name a few anyway: Jack Callahan, the teacher who first made me believe I could be a writer; John F. J. Sullivan, the editor who took a chance on a kid with no training and no experience and gave me my first byline; Bram Hepburn, with whom I have a cherished 30-year friendship; Tim O'Shei, my friend and mentor, who introduced me to my first book editor and opened the door for me to be here writing this book today; Dr. Michael I. Niman, the most influential professor of my collegiate career at Buffalo State College, whose classes made me both a better researcher and a stronger writer; my good friend Jerry Wohlleber, who offered invaluable late-night advice during this project, even if we still fiercely debate whether the G.O.A.T. is M. J. or LeBron (for the record, it's LeBron); my editor, David Lytle, and the team at Callisto Media; and finally, my mom, Christine Chandler. Though she left this world a year ago, the lessons she taught me and the love she gave me shape every word I write today. Without her, none of this would have ever been possible.

# ABOUT THE AUTHOR

**MATT CHANDLER** is the author of more than 55 nonfiction books. He writes extensively about all types of sports and athletes. His *Sports Illustrated Kids* book, *Side-by-Side Baseball Stars: Comparing the Game's Greatest Players*, was selected by the American Society of Journalists and Authors for its 2015 Young Adult Outstanding Book Award. Matt is a former newspaper journalist and six-time New York Press Association award-winner. He lives in New York with his wife, Amber; his children, Zoey and Ollie; and Lola the dog and Sam the bird. You can learn more about his work at mattchandlerwriting.com.

CPSIA information can be obtained
at www.ICGtesting.com
Printed in the USA
JSHW011445210520
5800JS00009B/35